AMBROSIA

Ambrosia is a Deep South mixture.
Oranges, sugar, cherries, pecans, and coconut.

Vicksburg is a Deep South mixture.
Italian, English, Lebanese, African, and Irish.

Ambrosia *is a Deep South mixture.*
Homes, recipes, and history.

First Printing 1997: 20,000 copies

Copyright © 1997 by the Junior Auxiliary of Vicksburg, Inc.
Vicksburg, Mississippi

Library of Congress Cataloging in Publication Data main entry under title
Ambrosia
97-60604

ISBN 0-9614988-1-1

Printed in the United States of America by Jostens

Also by the Junior Auxiliary of Vicksburg, Inc.
Vintage Vicksburg *(1985)*

All inquiries about this book or orders for additional copies should be directed to

JAV Publications
Post Office Box 86
Vicksburg, Mississippi, 39181-0086
601.634.1084

AMBROSIA

Photographs by Bob Pickett

Narratives by Brenda Ware Jones,
Martha Hickman Day,
Charlie Mitchell, Leslie Criss,
and Gordon Cotton

TABLE OF CONTENTS

Spring

Summer

Fall

Winter

DEDICATION

❖ ❖ ❖

We pray for children
  who bring us fistfuls of dandelions and sing off key,
  who have goldfish funerals, build card table forts,
  who slurp their cereal on purpose,
  who get gum in their hair, put sugar in their milk,
  who spit toothpaste all over the sink,
  who hug us for no reason, who bless us each night.

And we pray for those
  who never get dessert,
  who have no safe blanket to drag behind,
  who can't find any bread to steal,
  who don't have any rooms to clean up,
  whose pictures aren't on anybody's dresser,
  whose monsters are real.

We pray for children
  who want to be carried,
  and for those who must.
  For those we never give up on
  and for those who don't have a chance.
  For those we smother
  and those who will grab the hand of anybody
  kind enough to offer.

– Excerpt from the poem *A Prayer for Children*.

by Ina J. Hughes
Charleston, South Carolina

Your purchase of this book helps answer our prayers for children.

The Junior Auxiliary of Vicksburg was established in 1936 by twelve young women dedicated to helping children.
Since then, the members of the Junior Auxiliary of Vicksburg have spent countless hours teaching,
encouraging, playing with, rocking, singing to, and praying for children.

INTRODUCTION

❖ ❖ ❖

Ambrosia is defined as something that is exquisite to taste or smell. Greek mythology tells us it is the food of the gods. This ultimate food of celebration has been served at Southern celebrations for generations.

All Southerners live to celebrate; my family is no different. We chop and cook for days. Then we pull out Grandmother's china, polish silver, arrange flowers, and press table linens. We do all this because we know absolutely nothing is better than a day that begins with the house filling up with family. We know that as the day progresses, we'll eat way too much and listen to storytelling of the finest quality.

A holiday menu at our table is like ambrosia itself – an exquisite mixture of tastes and smells. We serve what we just 'have to have', like turkey and dressing and giblet gravy. Corn and potatoes are prepared to honor our Uncle Jack, who was a 'Yankee and proud of it!' For the children, we have a big dollop of marshmallow topping with just a little dab of sweet potato casserole hidden underneath. The marshmallow topping is, in fact, so prized that one of my more enterprising children once announced, "Only one square inch of marshmallow topping for everyone," thinking the rest would be his.

And last, but not least, comes the parade of

desserts. Mincemeat pies. Pecan pies. Charlotte Russe. And, of course, my mother's ambrosia. The very best.

As the day closes, we begin to plan the next time we'll all get together. There are hugs and kisses, and we stand in the driveway – even at the Governor's Mansion – and wave goodbye. The very best part of the day is still yet to come. It's when the house is quiet again and the last dish is put away. It's then we can reflect and relish the smell of the flowers, the texture of the tablecloth, the cold beads of water on our silver goblets, the pure joy of family all around. How exquisite everything was to taste and smell – ambrosia!

Pat Fordice

Pat Fordice
First Lady of Mississippi

Pat Fordice came to Vicksburg in 1962. In Vicksburg she and her husband Kirk Fordice raised their four children. She was an active volunteer in church and civic organizations, served as president of the Junior Auxiliary of Vicksburg, and became the gracious hostess who later captured the admiration of the entire state of Mississippi.

SPRING IN THE DEEP SOUTH

Springtime bursts onto the landscape of our Deep South like the gasp of first love – unexpected, almost despaired of, but quickly celebrated and imbibed! We Mississippians are no fools; we know a good (if ephemeral) thing when we see it. After those dull, gray, sodden winter months, we lose no time snatching the joy of those first daffodils. We're a lot like those cockeyed-optimist saucer magnolias, the early blooms of which always shrivel and drop during that one last cruel freeze which we never reckon on, and never will. For Southerners, spring is always just around the corner. It's the season we shine.

Spring is Pilgrimage, with the historical houses on proud parade, their old walnut and rosewood furniture polished to a scented gleam. Spring is the invigorating Run Thru History in the National Park. Spring is Riverfest, with loads of delicious street food and great loud music all over downtown. Spring is egg hunts at Eastertime, wedding brunches in lush garden settings, cocktails in cellar-temperature twilight on old-brick terraces with a sunset view of the Mighty Mississippi.

For those of us who grew up here, Vicksburg in the springtime is a lesson in *carpe diem*. We take our exquisite architecture, our cuisine, our beverages for granted – until we move away, assimilate ourselves into the outside world, and discover to our dismay that not everyone drinks a cold Co'-Cola for breakfast. Outsiders just don't understand. But we are delighted to teach them, and swarms of grateful tourists can testify that we do a pretty good job.

Any way you slice it, Spring is a glorious big pile of fun in the South. We dress in our snappiest new clothes, serve our most fabulous food, and spend every waking moment outdoors frolicking, gardening, and partying. For we know we must seize these days of crisp comfort – summer with its tropical heat will arrive all too soon.

Brenda Ware Jones

Brenda Ware Jones is an artist and writer. She is currently homes editor for Mississippi *magazine; her work has also appeared in* Southern Accents *and* The Clarion Ledger. *She now lives in Madison County with her husband, Edley Jones III, their daughter, Elizabeth, (also natives of Vicksburg) and assorted horses, dogs, and cats.*

All Saints' Episcopal School

"For All the Saints, who from their labors rest,
Who thee by faith before the world confessed,
Thy Name, O Jesus, be forever blessed –
Alleluia, Alleluia!"

The majestic tune of Ralph Vaughn Williams' mighty hymn has moved many an All Saints' alumnus to tears around graduation time. The grassy, shady Dell centered by the sparkling pool, the little chapel perched high on the hill, those massive Corinthian columns on the portico of Green Hall – all are part and parcel of many Saints' school-day memories.

Officially designated as "A Mission Station of the Episcopal Dioceses in Arkansas, Louisiana, and Mississippi," it is a very different place from the original All Saints' Episcopal College which welcomed fifty young ladies on September 16, 1909. Then, well-bred daughters of the diocese partook of a classical curriculum of Latin, Greek, French, piano, violin, and drawing, with a solid grounding in the great works of literature and higher mathematics. How shocked these young women would be today – and how delighted, probably – to find today's students studying physics and modern drama and sitting in front of computer screens.

And how would the original fifty have felt about the ultimate addition to the curriculum in 1970 – BOYS. The first seven male day students must have felt like foxes admitted to the henhouse, but apparently co-ed life was congenial – twenty years later, half of each graduating class was male and this remains true today.

In 1983, long-time school employee, Miss Mary Ellen Turner, compiled seventy-five years of All Saints' history in a volume appropriately titled *For All the Saints*. In the preface, the Most Reverend John Maury Allin ruefully notes that not everyone associated with the school has necessarily responded to the "call to be saints," set out in the New Testament books of Romans and Corinthians. True enough, any academic body will inevitably contain its share of devils as well as angels – a fact happily noted in the names of the school's two competing intramural teams. When points are tallied at the end of each year, sometimes the forces of dark (the Devils) come out ahead of those Angels of light – but so goes All Saints', so goes the world.

All Saints' Episcopal School, nestled in a bend of beautiful, verdant Confederate Avenue in Vicksburg, is proud of its location in an old, old town, the identity of which lies in its association with battle. Is this why one of the Saints' favorite old hymns is rich with combat imagery? Whatever the case, All Saints' will shine through the ages with accumulated glory from the Saints who have gone before, who have made it what it is today. May light perpetual shine upon them!

"O may thy soldiers, faithful, true, and bold,
Fight as the saints who nobly fought of old
And win, with them, the victor's crown of gold.
Alleluia, Alleluia!"

Brenda Ware Jones

GRADUATION BRUNCH

The speeches are over, the diplomas conferred, and the last student is driving away. Now it's time to celebrate! Honoring the commencement speaker and All Saints' very tired teachers is a unique brunch that reflects the recipes of years of entertaining Southern style.

Spring Cooler Punch
Magnolia Milk Punch
Shrimp and Crabmeat au Gratin
Asparagus Tart
Baked Tomatoes Rockefeller
Italian Cream Cake
Key Lime Pie
Cream Cheese Danish
Ambrosia

SPRING COOLER PUNCH

4 cups sugar
6 cups water
5 bananas
1 (6-ounce) can water
1 (12-ounce) can frozen orange juice
1 (6-ounce) can frozen lemonade
1 (42-ounce) can pineapple juice
3 quarts ginger ale

Boil sugar and 6 cups water in large saucepan for 3 minutes. Cool. Mash bananas in blender. Set aside. Combine can of water, orange juice, lemonade, pineapple juice, and bananas in a large bowl. Add sugar syrup; blend well. Freeze mixture for at least 24 hours. Remove mixture from freezer 1 hour before serving. Using a fork, break frozen punch into smaller pieces. Add ginger ale. Continue blending to a slushy consistency. Serve. **Yield: 50 punch cup servings.**

LEFT: **Spring Cooler Punch** in sterling silver English punch bowl.
ABOVE: **Desserts around the mahogany Chippendale dining room table from the rectory.**

13

MAGNOLIA MILK PUNCH

1 cup premium vanilla ice cream
1/4 cup bourbon
1 teaspoon vanilla
~ freshly grated nutmeg

Combine ice cream, bourbon, and vanilla in blender and process until smooth. Pour into glasses and sprinkle with nutmeg. **Yield: 2 servings.**

SHRIMP AND CRABMEAT AU GRATIN

1 medium onion, chopped
2 green onions, chopped
1 rib celery, chopped
1/2 cup butter
1/4 cup flour
1 cup half & half
1/4 cup dry white wine
1 tablespoon fresh parsley
1 egg, beaten
1 pound crabmeat
1 pound cooked, peeled shrimp
2 tablespoons grated Romano cheese
5 ounces grated cheddar cheese
1 teaspoon salt
1/4 teaspoon black pepper
1/4 teaspoon red pepper
1 1/2 teaspoons lemon juice
~ breadcrumbs

Sauté onions and celery in butter until soft. Stir in flour and add half & half slowly to make a smooth sauce. Remove from heat. Add white wine and stir to combine. Add remaining ingredients except breadcrumbs. Blend carefully and put in a 1 1/2-quart casserole dish. Top with breadcrumbs. Bake 20 minutes at 350°. **Yield: 6 to 8 servings.**

◆

ASPARAGUS TART

1 packaged pie crust
1 teaspoon flour
14 to 16 ounces fresh asparagus, each spear trimmed to 3 inches
2/3 cup half & half
2 eggs
1/2 cup freshly-grated Parmesan cheese
1 teaspoon dried tarragon
1/2 teaspoon salt
~ pepper to taste

Preheat oven to 450°. Fold out crust onto work surface. Repair any cracks. Dust lightly with flour. Arrange dough, flour side down, in a 9-inch tart pan with removable bottom. Press dough into pan. Fold excess dough over edge to form a double-thick side. Pierce dough all over with a fork. Bake until golden, about 15 minutes. Cool on rack. Reduce oven temperature to 375°. Cook asparagus in boiling water for 3 minutes. Drain well. Place on paper towels to absorb any excess water. Mix half & half, eggs, cheese, tarragon, and salt. Season with pepper. Arrange asparagus in tart pan, spoke fashion, with tips to the edge and cut ends meeting in center. Pour egg mixture over asparagus. Bake for 35 minutes or until tart puffs and top browns. Cool 5 minutes before serving. **Yield: 8 servings.**

SPRING IN THE DEEP SOUTH

BAKED TOMATOES ROCKEFELLER

2 (10-ounce) packages chopped spinach
1 medium onion, chopped
6 green onions, chopped
½ teaspoon minced garlic
½ cup olive oil or butter
6 eggs, slightly beaten
2 cups seasoned bread-crumbs, divided
¼ teaspoon Tabasco
¼ teaspoon Worcestershire sauce
1 teaspoon thyme
~ salt and pepper to taste
½ cup Parmesan cheese
12 thick tomato slices

Cook spinach according to package directions and set aside. Sauté all onions and garlic in olive oil. Remove from heat and set aside. To spinach, add eggs, 1 cup breadcrumbs, sautéed onions, Tabasco, Worcestershire sauce, seasonings, and cheese. Arrange tomato slices in a buttered baking dish. Mound spinach mixture onto each slice. Sprinkle with remaining breadcrumbs. Bake at 350° for 15 minutes. May be prepared a day before baking. Spinach mixture freezes well. **Yield: 12 servings.**

OPPOSITE PAGE, TOP FAR LEFT: **Asparagus Tart.** OPPOSITE PAGE, TOP LEFT: **Cloistered passageway between campus buildings.** OPPOSITE PAGE, BOTTOM: **View of Green Hall.** ABOVE: **Baked Tomatoes Rockefeller.** RIGHT: **Graduation Brunch on the columned gallery of Green Hall.**

All Saints' Episcopal School

ITALIAN CREAM CAKE

Cake:
- 1 stick butter
- 1/2 cup shortening
- 2 cups sugar
- 5 eggs, separated
- 1 cup buttermilk
- 1 teaspoon soda
- 2 cups all-purpose flour
- 1 teaspoon vanilla
- 1 cup chopped pecans
- 1 (3.5-ounce) can of coconut
- ~ Frosting

Preheat oven to 325°. Grease and flour 3 (8-inch) cake pans. Set aside. Cream butter, shortening, and sugar. Add egg yolks one at a time, blending well after each addition. Mix together buttermilk and soda. Add flour and buttermilk alternately to butter mixture, ending with flour. Beat egg whites. Fold in egg whites, vanilla, pecans, and coconut. Divide batter evenly among cake pans. Bake at 325° for 40 minutes. Let cool completely before frosting.

Frosting:
- 1 stick butter
- 1 (8-ounce) package cream cheese
- 1 teaspoon vanilla
- 1 box powdered sugar

Cream butter, cream cheese, and vanilla. Gradually add powdered sugar.

KEY LIME PIE

- 1 1/4 cups graham cracker crumbs (11 full crackers)
- 3 tablespoons sugar
- 5 tablespoons butter, melted
- 4 teaspoons grated lime zest
- 4 large egg yolks
- 1 (14-ounce) can sweetened condensed milk
- 1/2 cup fresh lime juice, strained (3 to 4 limes)
- 3/4 cup heavy cream
- 1/3 cup powdered sugar
- 1/2 lime sliced paper thin and dipped in sugar for garnish

Preheat oven to 325°. Mix crumbs and sugar. Add butter and stir with a fork until combined. Put mixture into a 9-inch pie plate. Press crumbs over bottom and sides to form an even crust. Bake for 15 minutes. Cool on wire rack to room temperature. Whisk zest and egg yolks in a medium bowl until mixture is tinted light green, about 2 minutes. Beat in condensed milk. Beat in lime juice. Set aside to thicken at room temperature. Pour filling into crust. Bake for 15 minutes. Return pie to wire racks and cool to room temperature. Refrigerate until well chilled, at least 3 hours. Up to 2 hours before serving, whip cream to soft peaks. Add powdered sugar, one tablespoon at a time, and continue beating until just-stiff peaks form. Pipe whipped cream over filling or spread evenly with a spatula. Garnish with sugared lime slices.

TOP: **Cream Cheese Danish, Key Lime Pie, and Magnolia Milk Punch.**
BOTTOM: **Gargoyle-based table and desserts.**
OPPOSITE PAGE, TOP: **Corinthian-columned rectory built in 1950.**
OPPOSITE PAGE, BOTTOM: **Ambrosia in orange cups.**

CREAM CHEESE DANISH

- 2 packages refrigerated crescent rolls
- 2 (8-ounce) packages cream cheese
- 2 cups sugar, divided
- 1 egg
- 1 teaspoon vanilla
- 1 cup pecans, chopped
- 1/2 cup butter, melted

Preheat oven to 350°. Grease a 9 x 13 x 2-inch baking dish. Unroll one can of crescent rolls and press into the bottom of the pan, pinching perforations closed. Combine cream cheese, 1 1/2 cups sugar, egg, and vanilla. Beat until smooth and creamy. Spread cream cheese mixture over dough. Unroll second can of dough and place over cream cheese mixture. Combine 1/2 cup sugar and pecans in food processor. Process until pecans are finely chopped. Spread pecans over top layer of dough. Drizzle with melted butter. Bake 30 minutes or until golden brown. May be served warm or cold.

AMBROSIA

6 cups halved orange sections, seeds and membranes removed

3 cups fresh pineapple, chopped

3 cups fresh coconut, shredded

1½ cups maraschino cherries, halved, drained, and rinsed

¾ cup pecans, chopped

~ powdered sugar to taste

Combine all ingredients in a large bowl. Cover and refrigerate. **Yield: 12 servings.**

Every town must have its own very best story. In Vicksburg that story is, hands down, The Chicken Salad Story. It has been told over and over with slightly different twists and turns; and it has even appeared in magazine stories and most recently in a novel set in another Southern town. But it happened right here in Vicksburg in the 1950s on Chambers Street at the home of our one and only Ann Andrews. My mother was there and she told me the whole story word for word.

There were nine ladies in the Tuesday Bridge Club who would get together at each other's homes at about ten in the morning and play cards until twelve or twelve-thirty, depending on how the cards were going; and then they would stop for a nice lunch. Back then, the hostess didn't even play cards – she just cooked and served and kept everybody happy. On this particular summer day on Chambers Street, Ann happily decorated her plates for tomatoes stuffed with chicken salad and went to the living room to announce, "Girls, come on to the table." When she returned to the kitchen she was horrified by what she saw – her cat, eating out of the bowl of chicken salad! She was faced with an enormous dilemma – to serve or not to serve. Being that eight women were now seated at her dining room table with just a glass of iced tea, she decided to serve. She scooped out what appeared to be the disturbed portion and stuffed those tomatoes fast. She tried to appear cool, calm, and collected as she served her pretty plates and said, "Girls, do try my chicken salad." She then retreated to the kitchen to check on the rolls, and what she saw on that trip horrified her even more than the last. This time, out of the kitchen window, she saw her cat again, but stretched out dead. She racked her brain of what to say as she flew back to the dining room. Coming up with no explanation, she simply said, "Girls, don't eat the chicken salad." While the girls' forks were still hanging in midair, the telephone rang. Thankful for a reprieve, Ann answered it. It was her neighbor, Pauline Biedenharn, apologizing profusely because she had run over Ann's cat. Ann said, "Oh, darling, that's all right," and then returned to her guests. She simply said to her utterly confused friends, "Girls, you can eat the chicken salad now." No one in Vicksburg will ever forget that story or our dear, lovable Ann.

David Hunt Dabney

All Saints' Episcopal School

Duff Green Mansion

Duff Green Mansion was built as a wedding present by prosperous, local merchant Duff Green for his wife Mary on a parcel of land given to them by her parents, Judge and Mrs. William Lake. This is a house that has witnessed the best and worst of Vicksburg history since its construction began in 1856.

Its four-story facade is Italianate with the flat roof and ornate iron balustrades that define the style. In its very earliest days as a family residence, Duff Green looked much as it does today. Mary and Duff Green gave glittering parties and welcomed Sunday luncheon guests in a style befitting genteel young Vicksburgers of patrician birth. But things began going downhill rapidly while the house was still practically new. A most inconvenient thing happened to interrupt the pleasures of daily social life in this 12,000-square-foot mansion – war.

During the Siege of Vicksburg in 1863, the house was used as a hospital for wounded soldiers, while the family went to live around the corner at Lakemont with Mary's parents. When the shells began falling in the streets during the heat of the battle, the family fled to the deeper shelter of a cave in one of the nearby hills. A pregnant Mary Green, perhaps thrown into labor by the noise and horror all around her, gave birth to a son in that cave – and named him (what else?) Siege.

Legend has it that injured Union soldiers were bedded in the house's third-floor bedrooms, with the Confederate wounded occupying the lower stories. A penthouse river view for the Yankees? Hardly. The reason for this was quite pragmatic. The local doctors figured that if the Yankees dropped an exploding shell onto the house, they would blow up some of their own first.

The iron balconies were ripped off and melted down for ammunition by the desperate, non-industrial South, which salvaged iron where it could. After the Civil War the mansion sat forlorn and stripped of its ornaments, like a woman forced to pawn her jewels. Sold in 1880, it was for years an orphaned boys' home; then in 1932 it became the headquarters for the local Salvation Army. Painted a sickly hospital-green (a decorative pun on its name and wartime function?), it was the object of many a Vicksburger's staid comment, "If only someone would buy that place and fix it up..."

In 1985 Alicia and Harry Sharp did just that, and did a knockout period-restoration on the derelict, old mansion. Now a splendidly furnished bed and breakfast, the Duff Green is once more the proud, gay hostess of lavish soirees, festive dinners, and elegant charity balls.

Vicksburgers are grateful that this lovely place escaped demolition and has survived to show new generations the meaning of endurance and grace under fire.

Brenda Ware Jones

EASTER BUFFET

*Remember the magic of finding a beautiful Easter egg?
Most adults never discover anything to equal it. But
those lucky few who feast their eyes and palates on this
fabulous Fabergé-style cake will once again want to
scream, "I found it!"*

Frosted Baby Greens
Leg of Lamb with Mint Pesto
Carrot Soufflé
Asparagus Dijonnaise
Lemon Cheesecake with Fresh Berries
Fabergé-Egg Cake

FROSTED BABY GREENS

2 bags baby greens or other spring salad greens
1 cup heavy cream
2 tablespoons sugar
1/4 teaspoon salt
1/4 cup wine vinegar
1 cup walnuts, chopped

Place greens in large bowl. Whip cream with sugar and salt until mixture begins to thicken. Stir in vinegar. Pour dressing over greens. Toss in walnuts and serve immediately. **Yield: 10 to 12 servings.**

LEFT: The central hall opening onto the back gallery. RIGHT: Frosted Baby Greens served on Kan Sou by Puiforcat. Sterling silver flatware is Buttercup by Gorham. Crystal is Avoca by Waterford. Daffodils in a sterling biscuit barrel.

LEG OF LAMB WITH MINT PESTO

LEG OF LAMB:

2 teaspoons salt
2 teaspoons pepper
1 teaspoon finely-minced, fresh rosemary leaves or ½ teaspoon dried
1 (5 to 6 pound) leg of lamb, hip bone removed, rolled and tied by butcher
2 cloves garlic, peeled and slivered into 8 pieces
2 tablespoons olive oil
~ Mint Pesto

Mix salt, pepper, and rosemary. Cut slits into lamb with sharp knife and insert a garlic sliver into each slit. Rub seasoning mixture over all surfaces of the lamb. Brush with olive oil. Place leg, top side up, on a roasting pan fitted with a wire rack. Let stand for 30 minutes. Meanwhile, adjust oven rack to lowest level and heat oven to 450°. Roast lamb for 10 minutes. Grasp shank bone with paper towels and flip leg over and continue roasting. Turn leg every 20 minutes until an instant-read thermometer inserted in several locations registers 130° to 135°, about 60 to 80 minutes. Remove leg from oven and cover with foil. Let stand for 20 minutes before carving. Serve with Mint Pesto. **Yield: 6 to 8 servings.**

MINT PESTO:

2¼ cups packed fresh mint leaves
1 cup packed fresh parsley
½ cup walnuts
2 cloves garlic
¾ to 1 cup olive oil
6 tablespoons fresh lime juice
5 teaspoons sugar
1½ teaspoons salt

Combine mint, parsley, walnuts, and garlic in bowl of food processor fitted with metal blade. Process to a paste. Gradually add olive oil through feed tube and process until smooth. Add lime juice, sugar, and salt. Process to combine. Serve immediately or store in refrigerator in airtight container.

TOP LEFT: **Herend bunny and hand-painted eggs.** TOP RIGHT: **Asparagus Dijonnaise, Leg of Lamb with Mint Pesto, and Carrot Soufflé.** BOTTOM: **Leg of Lamb.**

SPRING IN THE DEEP SOUTH

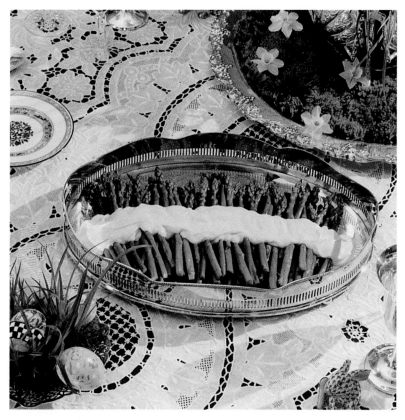

LEMON CHEESECAKE WITH FRESH BERRIES

4   (8-ounce) packages cream cheese
1   cup sugar
1   tablespoon orange-flavored liqueur or orange juice
4   eggs
1   cup sour cream
7   tablespoons fresh lemon juice
2   tablespoons grated lemon peel
1   pint seasonal berries
1/4 cup apricot preserves
1 1/2 tablespoons water

Preheat oven to 300°. Generously grease a 9-inch springform pan. Beat cream cheese until light. Add sugar and liqueur and beat until thoroughly combined. Add eggs, one at a time, beating well after each addition. Fold in sour cream, lemon juice, and lemon peel. Pour into prepared pan. Bake until outside is set, but center moves slightly when shaken, about 1 hour and 15 minutes. Cool on wire rack. Cover with plastic wrap and refrigerate overnight. Release pan sides and place cheesecake on a serving platter. Mound desired berries in center of cheesecake leaving a 1-inch border. Heat preserves with water in small saucepan, stirring until melted. Brush warm glaze over berries. **Yield: 10 servings.**

CARROT SOUFFLÉ

2   pounds carrots, cooked and mashed
1/2 cup butter
2   eggs, beaten
3   tablespoons flour
1   teaspoon baking powder
3/4 cup sugar
1   pinch cinnamon

Combine all ingredients and pour into a buttered, 2-quart soufflé dish. Bake at 400° for 15 minutes. Reduce heat to 350° and bake an additional 45 minutes. **Yield: 6 to 8 servings.**

ASPARAGUS DIJONNAISE

3   pounds fresh asparagus, trimmed
1   cup mayonnaise
2   tablespoons Dijon mustard
1   teaspoon lemon juice

Steam asparagus until spears turn bright green and are barely tender, 4 to 6 minutes. Rinse in cold water to stop the cooking process. Mix mayonnaise, Dijon mustard, and lemon juice. Serve asparagus with sauce for dipping or spoon sauce over asparagus spears when serving on a plate.

TOP: **Asparagus Dijonnaise.**
RIGHT: **Lemon Cheesecake with Fresh Berries.**

Duff Green Mansion

FABERGÉ-EGG CAKE

2 (12-inch) square sheets butter cake or genoise baked 1½ inches thick
1 (14-inch) square sheet and 2 (12-inch) square sheets chocolate butter cake, baked 1½ inches thick
~ Simple Rum Syrup
~ Chocolate Hazelnut Praline Truffle Filling
~ Deep Chocolate Ganache
~ Apricot Glaçage
~ Chocolate Glaçage
~ a variety of colored buttercreams
~ satin ribbons for garnish
~ fresh grass sod or Easter grass for presentation
1 (14 x 12-inch) flat egg pattern cut out of lightweight cardboard

Bake the cakes and chill well for easy handling. On a cardboard or wooden base covered with foil, work quickly and assemble cake as follows:

1. Start with 1 (12-inch) butter cake.
2. Brush with Simple Rum Syrup.
3. Spread thickly with Chocolate Hazelnut Praline Truffle Filling.
4. Top with the 14-inch chocolate cake.
5. Brush with Simple Rum Syrup.
6. Spread with Deep Chocolate Ganache.
7. Top with second 12-inch butter cake.
8. Lay the cardboard egg pattern on the cake and cut around it.

Remove the pattern.

9. Brush last layer with Simple Rum Syrup.
10. Spread thickly with Chocolate Hazelnut Praline Truffle Filling.
11. Top with 1 (12-inch) chocolate cake.
12. Top with a piece of aluminum foil and chill for at least 4 hours.
13. Remove cake from refrigerator.

Place a second cardboard or wooden base on top and turn the cake over to complete the assembly. A 12-inch butter cake will be facing up.

14. Brush top layer with Simple Rum Syrup.
15. Spread with Deep Chocolate Ganache.
16. Top with the last 12-inch chocolate square. Chill for 20 minutes.

Now comes the freehand shaping. It is important to work quickly and carefully.

17. Using an electric knife, roughly shape the top and bottom layers.
18. Cover with plastic wrap and chill for at least 2 hours before final shaping.
19. Unwrap the egg. Using an electric knife, carefully pare and cut to achieve a smooth egg shape.

It is important to leave a broad enough portion of the base to support the weight of the entire cake. You can undercut both ends of the bottom of the egg for shape and still leave a solid base. The grass will hide the flat portion of the bottom.

20. Brush entire cake with a thin layer of Apricot Glaçage to seal the cake in preparation for the final coverings. Allow glaçage to dry for 10 minutes.
21. Spread entire cake with a thin layer of Deep Chocolate Ganache. Chill for 20 minutes.
22. Spread entire cake with a generous layer of Hazelnut Praline Truffle Filling. Chill while you are preparing the Chocolate Glaçage.
23. On rack over a pan lined with plastic wrap, pour an even layer of room-temperature Chocolate Glaçage over entire cake in one motion to insure a smooth surface. You can slightly tip and shake the cake to distribute the glaçage. Chill until you are ready to decorate.
24. Decorate the egg with elegant filigree and whimsical designs using the various colored buttercreams.
25. Tie the egg with ribbon and top with a bow. Position on a silver tray covered with fresh moss and grass or Easter grass.

SIMPLE RUM SYRUP

1 cup sugar
3/4 cup water
1/2 cup light rum

Dissolve sugar in water in a small saucepan. Bring to a boil. Simmer 5 minutes. Remove from heat and stir in rum. Simple Rum Syrup can be stored indefinitely in the refrigerator.

CHOCOLATE HAZELNUT PRALINE TRUFFLE FILLING

1½ cups heavy whipping cream
½ cup unsalted butter
1 pound highest quality milk chocolate or semisweet chocolate, broken into pieces
1 tablespoon hazelnut liqueur
¾ cup Hazelnut Praline Powder

Bring cream and butter to a boil. Add chocolate and cover for 10 minutes. Stir until completely smooth and free of lumps. Add liqueur and cool to room temperature for 2 hours. Chill 30 minutes. Using an electric mixer, beat until light and fluffy. Add Hazelnut Praline Powder and mix well.

HAZELNUT PRALINE POWDER

1 cup sugar
2 tablespoons water
2 tablespoons butter
1 teaspoon cinnamon
1 cup hazelnuts, toasted

In a heavy skillet melt the sugar and water until sugar is a rich amber. Add butter and cinnamon. Stir to combine. Add hazelnuts and stir to combine. Pour out on foil-lined cookie sheet which has been sprayed with no-stick cooking spray. Allow to cool and harden. Break praline into manageable pieces and process in food processor. This mixture can be added to cakes, ice cream, fillings, cookies, etc.

DEEP CHOCOLATE GANACHE

1 cup heavy whipping cream
8 ounces semisweet chocolate

Scald cream in heavy saucepan over medium heat. Add chocolate and stir until melted and well blended. Let cool.

APRICOT GLAÇAGE

2 (10-ounce) jars apricot jam
½ cup sugar
½ cup water

Combine jam, sugar, and water in a small saucepan and stir over low heat until smooth. Push sauce through a sieve with a spoon. Let cool.

CHOCOLATE GLAÇAGE

18 ounces of good, imported milk chocolate or dark chocolate, broken into small pieces
1½ cups unsalted butter
3 tablespoons light corn syrup
1 tablespoon vanilla extract

Melt chocolate, butter, and corn syrup in microwave. Stir until smooth. Add vanilla and stir well. There must be no lumps. Cool slightly. Use immediately.

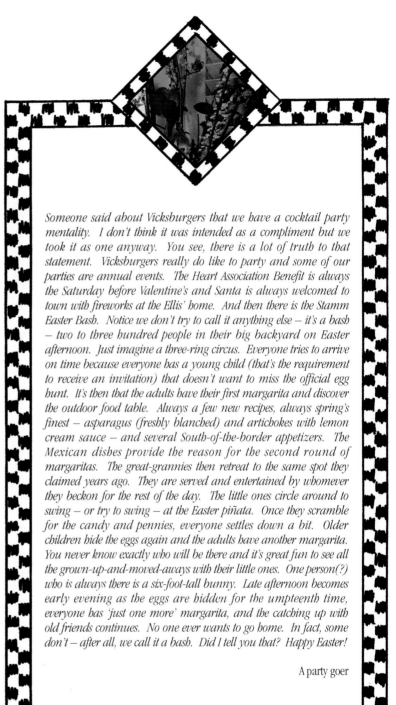

Someone said about Vicksburgers that we have a cocktail party mentality. I don't think it was intended as a compliment but we took it as one anyway. You see, there is a lot of truth to that statement. Vicksburgers really do like to party and some of our parties are annual events. The Heart Association Benefit is always the Saturday before Valentine's and Santa is always welcomed to town with fireworks at the Ellis' home. And then there is the Stamm Easter Bash. Notice we don't try to call it anything else – it's a bash – two to three hundred people in their big backyard on Easter afternoon. Just imagine a three-ring circus. Everyone tries to arrive on time because everyone has a young child (that's the requirement to receive an invitation) that doesn't want to miss the official egg hunt. It's then that the adults have their first margarita and discover the outdoor food table. Always a few new recipes, always spring's finest – asparagus (freshly blanched) and artichokes with lemon cream sauce – and several South-of-the-border appetizers. The Mexican dishes provide the reason for the second round of margaritas. The great-grannies then retreat to the same spot they claimed years ago. They are served and entertained by whomever they beckon for the rest of the day. The little ones circle around to swing – or try to swing – at the Easter piñata. Once they scramble for the candy and pennies, everyone settles down a bit. Older children hide the eggs again and the adults have another margarita. You never know exactly who will be there and it's great fun to see all the grown-up-and-moved-aways with their little ones. One person(?) who is always there is a six-foot-tall bunny. Late afternoon becomes early evening as the eggs are hidden for the umpteenth time, everyone has 'just one more' margarita, and the catching up with old friends continues. No one ever wants to go home. In fact, some don't – after all, we call it a bash. Did I tell you that? Happy Easter!

A party goer

The Vicksburg National Military Park

The hills. Oh, those bloody hills.

The Battlefield, as the 1,700 acres of manicured, emerald-green turf are known locally, looks nothing like it did in 1863. Then, heavy Dahlgren cannons dug ruts in the mud, and cussing soldiers atop screaming horses churned over the rolling landscape. All in a desperate, doomed attempt to save their beloved bluff town and put a kink in Abe Lincoln's plans. These hills, some almost surreal in their sudden steepness, are now topped with huge marble, granite, and bronze monuments.

The Vicksburg National Military Park, as it was officially christened by an Act of Congress in 1899, is a haunting place, particularly at twilight. Some say it is quite literally haunted. The Five Faces on the Pennsylvania Monument are said to cry blood at midnight; the statue of General Ulysses S. Grant, astride his horse Kangaroo, is said to come alive during every full moon and ride around the old battlefield. Loyal, unreconstructed Confederates, even today, feel a vicious delight that the old Yankee hypocrite isn't resting easy in his grave, though it seems unfair to the horse to pull eternal sentry duty.

The Park – that eerie, hilly terrain – etches its image into the very soul of anyone who spends much time there. If you grow up in Vicksburg, you carry it with you forever. When you read Henry V's declamation on St. Crispin's Day, you don't picture Agincourt (sorry, Mr. Shakespeare), but Fort Nogales and the sweeping view over Lake Centennial. When you read the war poetry of Rupert Brooke, you don't envisage Ypres or the poppies on Flanders Field, but the National Cemetery. This vast graveyard with its ancient magnolias and endless rows of white tombstones is as sad a place as you can find anywhere.

Ushered into the cool darkness of the theater of the Visitors Center, watching that eighteen-minute film about the Siege of Vicksburg, a somber mood settles on anyone with an ounce of sensibility. How could those brave Southern fellows stand to hunker down in steamy trenches and fool with ramrods, gunpowder, and muzzle-loaders – then get their britches shot off, their trusty mounts blown out from under them, when all around them the woods were in flower and the honeysuckle was blooming?

What local child hasn't run up and down the grassy slope leading upwards to the Shirley House? Or shouted up into the rotunda of the massive Illinois monument to hear the spooky echoes? What adult watching the annual costumed re-enactment of the Siege doesn't feel a nameless thrill?

The Park is no battleground today; it is a vast, beautifully kept, public sanctuary, peopled, not by warring soldiers, but by tourists from all over the world. They arrive brandishing 35mm cameras instead of swords, toiling on foot up the steep inclines. Local joggers and walkers spend lots of time there as well, paying homage to the unforgiving hills.

Those hills. Those bloody hills.

Brenda Ware Jones

RUN THRU HISTORY PICNIC

The old saying, "As easy as a walk in the park," has never made a particle of sense to anyone in Vicksburg. The National Military Park boasts the town's steepest and most difficult hills, which made the park the natural choice for joggers when the Run Thru History began in 1980. Vicksburg volunteers put on a run and a walk that attract brave people from all over the country.

Roasted Garlic and Sun-Dried Tomato Cream Cheese
Caramelized Bacon and Turkey Sandwiches
Greek Pasta Salad
Artichokes with Lemon Butter Sauce
Chocolate Cherry Cake
White Chocolate Oatmeal Cookies

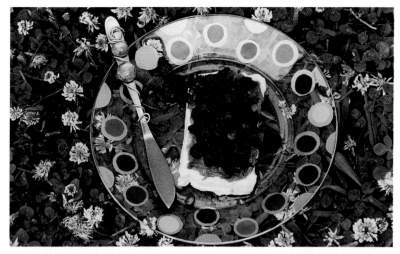

ROASTED GARLIC AND SUN-DRIED TOMATO CREAM CHEESE

1 head garlic
~ olive oil
1 (8-ounce) carton light cream cheese
1/4 cup oil-packed, sun-dried tomatoes, drained and chopped
1/4 teaspoon cayenne pepper
1 tablespoon green onion tops, chopped

Cut the top off of the head of garlic. Drizzle with olive oil and bake at 250° to 300° for 30 to 40 minutes or until garlic is soft. Squeeze out garlic and mash. Unmold cream cheese from carton and place on a serving plate. Top with roasted garlic, sun-dried tomatoes, cayenne pepper, and green onions. Serve with your favorite crackers.

CARAMELIZED BACON AND TURKEY SANDWICHES

1 1/2 cups brown sugar, packed
1 pound bacon
8 onion rolls
~ mayonnaise
1 pound sliced turkey
8 tomato slices
8 leaves of lettuce
~ salt and pepper to taste

Preheat oven to 350°. Place sugar in a shallow pan. Add strips of bacon, one at a time, and completely coat with sugar. Place on a large broiler pan or on a rack set over a rimmed baking sheet. Bake until bacon is dark golden brown, turning once, about 8 minutes on each side. Using tongs, transfer bacon to rack and cool. Can be prepared 4 hours ahead. To assemble sandwiches, spread mayonnaise on onion rolls, top with turkey, bacon, a tomato slice, and a leaf of lettuce. Add salt and pepper. **Yield:** 8 sandwiches.

LEFT: Picnic lunch on floor cloth by Suzanne Foster of Jackson, Mississippi.
TOP: Roasted Garlic and Sun-Dried Tomato Cream Cheese on hand-painted plate by Kaffie Hervey. Spreader by North River Studio of Meridian, Mississippi.

ARTICHOKES WITH LEMON BUTTER SAUCE

6   fresh artichokes
12   lemon slices
1   tablespoon olive oil
~   dash of salt
~   dash of pepper
2   dashes Tabasco
~   Lemon Butter Sauce

Spread leaves of artichokes apart and run cold water into them to wash off any grit. Slice the top inch off the cone of leaves with a serrated knife. Clip the top 1/2-inch of the remaining leaves with kitchen shears. Cut off the stem of the artichoke even with the base. Place a lemon slice on the top and bottom of each artichoke and secure with string. Fill a large kettle with about 1 to 2 inches of water. Season with olive oil, salt, pepper, and Tabasco. Bring to a boil. Reduce heat and boil for 45 minutes or until artichokes are tender. Drain, cover, and refrigerate overnight. Serve with Lemon Butter Sauce.

LEMON BUTTER SAUCE:

1   cup melted butter
~   lemon juice to taste
~   salt and pepper to taste

Combine all ingredients and mix well.
Yield: 1 cup.

GREEK PASTA SALAD

1   (12-ounce) package rainbow rotini
2   cucumbers, peeled and chopped
1   pint cherry tomatoes, quartered
1   bunch green onions, chopped
2   (14-ounce) cans artichoke hearts, drained and quartered
1   jar kalamata olives, drained and pitted
1   (8-ounce) package feta cheese, crumbled
1/4 cup olive oil
3/4 cup red wine vinegar
1   teaspoon dry mustard
2   teaspoons garlic powder
1   teaspoon black pepper
1/2 teaspoon salt

Cook pasta according to package directions. Drain and rinse. Combine pasta, cucumbers, tomatoes, onions, artichokes, olives, and feta cheese in a large bowl. In small bowl, combine olive oil, vinegar, mustard, garlic powder, pepper, and salt. Whisk to combine. Pour over pasta mixture and toss. Chill and serve. Can be made ahead. **Yield: 12 servings.**

CHOCOLATE CHERRY CAKE

1   box butter fudge cake mix
2   eggs, beaten
1   (21-ounce) can cherry pie filling
1   teaspoon almond extract
~   Fudge Frosting

Combine all ingredients except frosting in a large bowl and mix with wooden spoon. Pour into a greased and floured bundt pan. Bake at 350° for 30 minutes. Let cool for 15 minutes. Turn cake out onto a cake plate. Let cool completely. Spoon warm Fudge Frosting onto top of bundt cake, letting any extra frosting spill over into the middle. Let cool.
Yield: 10 to 12 servings.

FUDGE FROSTING:

1   cup sugar
1/3 cup milk
5   tablespoons margarine
1   (6-ounce) bag semisweet chocolate chips
1   teaspoon vanilla

Combine sugar, milk, and margarine in a small saucepan. Stir until margarine melts. Bring to a boil and boil 1 minute. Add chocolate chips and vanilla and stir until chips are melted. Let frosting cool for about 20 minutes, stirring regularly, until frosting begins to thicken.

TOP LEFT: Artichokes with Lemon Butter Sauce in serving pieces by potter Shane Peyton. BOTTOM, FAR LEFT: Battery DeGolyer. From here, a battery of guns hammered the Confederate Great Redoubt. BOTTOM LEFT: The Shirley House, the only surviving wartime structure in the Park. TOP: Spectacular view from the Illinois monument. BOTTOM: Texas monument.

WHITE CHOCOLATE OATMEAL COOKIES

- 2 sticks unsalted butter, softened
- 1 cup light brown sugar, packed
- 1 cup sugar
- 2 eggs
- 1½ cups all-purpose flour
- ½ teaspoon salt
- ½ teaspoon baking powder
- ¼ teaspoon nutmeg
- 3 cups oatmeal, original or quick-cooking
- 1 cup raisins
- ½ cup pecans, coarsely chopped
- 1 (12-ounce) package white chocolate chips

Adjust oven racks to low and middle positions. Preheat oven to 350°. Beat butter until creamy with electric mixer. Add sugars and beat until fluffy, about 3 minutes. Beat in eggs, one at a time. Mix flour, salt, baking powder, and nutmeg together. Mix flour mixture into butter mixture. Add oats, raisins, pecans, and white chocolate chips. Mix thoroughly. Line two large baking sheets with parchment paper. Form dough into 16 to 20 two-inch balls. Place dough balls onto cookie sheets and bake until cookie edges turn golden brown, 22 to 25 minutes. Halfway during baking, turn cookie sheets from front to back and switch from top to bottom. **Yield:** 16 to 20 large cookies.

ABOVE: **Greek Pasta Salad and Chocolate Cherry Cake** in pottery by Shane Peyton. RIGHT TOP: **Alabama monument.** RIGHT CENTER: **Entrance arch.** BELOW: **Twenty oxen pull the boulder for the Massachusetts monument in 1903.** J. Mack Moore photograph.

The Vicksburg National Military Park

27

Cameron Place

For years it was known as the old Morrissey house, and even today locals of a certain vintage still refer to Cameron Place that way. Despite its former name, Captain Tom Morrissey wasn't the original owner. Morrissey, an orphaned Irish immigrant who made his fortune in Vicksburg, bought the house in 1907 from Regina Hirsch. Before that, it had changed hands several times since around 1830, when it was built as a small, two-room dwelling. Today it is the home of David and Cheryl Cameron and their daughter Elizabeth.

Dr. A. L. Magruder bought the place in 1851 and built a larger house on the property for use as his residence and office. The facade in those days had none of the Italianate embellishments it wears today; it was a dignified Colonial-style house with Federal features. It was, and remains, a solid structure – the exterior walls are three bricks thick.

In 1869 it was sold to a man named Nathaniel Thomas. "We think he was probably a carpetbagger," muses Cheryl Cameron, referring to a certain class of post-war Northern opportunists that descended like a flock of vultures on the conquered South to make fast money off the region. They came from obscurity, with not much more than they could tote in a carpetbag, but many amassed great wealth in the boom days of Reconstruction. "Certainly no Southerner around that time would have been able to afford such a big house. It was Mr. Thomas who 'Italianated' the place, adding the porch, ornate brackets, and quoins in the fashion of the period."

"Captain Tom" bought the house from Mrs. Hirsch, who had purchased it from Nathaniel Thomas. When his heirs sold it to Cheryl and David, it was definitely in need of repair. The rear parlor floor sagged so badly that it had to be torn out and replaced. An entire two-story, wooden, lean-to addition on the back of the house had to come down. Once it was gone, the Camerons realized that all the plumbing had been in that derelict wing.

Once the structure was whole and functional, the artwork began. There were exquisitely detailed, plaster ceiling medallions to be restored and bronze gaslight chandeliers that had to be painstakingly taken apart and polished. Cheryl wanted the thirteen-foot-tall pier mirror moved from the dining room to the central hall, a simple-sounding process that ended up taking eleven men; it weighs over a thousand pounds.

The Camerons have added a long kitchen and guest wing behind the house, as well as a pool and gardens. It is, they stress, their private home rather than a showplace, though they generously welcome Pilgrimage guests each season.

Time and circumstance work inevitable changes on a house. Many owners, fashions, political climates, and styles of living have come and gone at 1117 Cherry Street since the 1830s; but one thing has remained a constant – it was built as a family home for comfort rather than ostentation, and so it has remained. Even that carpetbagger couldn't alter its architectural integrity.

Brenda Ware Jones

SUNDAY DINNER

For many years in Vicksburg the only place to have Sunday dinner was the Old Southern Tea Room. The smell of good food and the voices of good friends will linger on in the minds of those who ate there. Mary McKay, founder of the Tea Room, was kind enough to leave us with her best recipes, which are to this day re-created, especially on Sundays, in Vicksburg homes.

Frozen Apricot Salad
Oven-Fried Chicken
Old South Corn Pudding
New South String Beans
Sunday Squash
Coconut Cake with Pineapple Filling

TOP: **Painting by David Cameron's grandfather, O. B. Humma.**
BOTTOM: **Italianate bracketing.**
ABOVE: **Dining room.** RIGHT: **Frozen Apricot Salad and Iced Tea.**

FROZEN APRICOT SALAD

1   (12-ounce) can frozen orange juice concentrate
1   juice can water
1   cup sugar
1   (16-ounce) can apricots, drained
1   (20-ounce) can crushed pineapple, drained
6   medium bananas, cubed
~   curly leaf lettuce

Line 36 standard muffin cups with foil liners. Set aside. Mix frozen orange juice, water, and sugar. Stir until combined. Chop apricots into small pieces. Add apricots, pineapples, and bananas to juice. Divide mixture among the muffin cups and freeze overnight. Store frozen salads in large plastic bags until ready to serve. Salads keeps several weeks in freezer. Before serving, peel off liner and place on a bed of curly leaf lettuce. **Yield: 36 salads.**

OVEN-FRIED CHICKEN

8 boneless, skinless chicken breasts
1 cup buttermilk baking mix
½ teaspoon Creole seasoning
1 teaspoon paprika
½ cup pecans, finely chopped
3 eggs, beaten
½ teaspoon salt
¼ teaspoon pepper
1 cup all-purpose flour
½ cup butter, melted

Preheat oven to 350°. Wash chicken breasts and pat dry with paper towels. Combine baking mix, Creole seasoning, paprika, and pecans. Mix well and set aside. Mix eggs, salt, and pepper. Set aside. Roll each chicken breast in flour. Dip each breast in egg wash and roll in baking mix mixture. Place chicken in a greased 9 x 13 x 2-inch baking pan. Drizzle with butter. Bake uncovered for 1 hour. **Yield: 8 servings.**

OLD SOUTH CORN PUDDING

2 (15-ounce) cans cream-style corn
2 tablespoons sugar
1 teaspoon salt
3 tablespoons butter, melted
5 eggs, well beaten
1 cup milk
1 tablespoon cornstarch
1 tablespoon cold water

Preheat oven to 350°. Combine corn, sugar, salt, butter, eggs, and milk. Dissolve cornstarch in water and stir into corn mixture. Pour into a greased, shallow 2-quart baking dish. Bake for 1

hour or until corn mixture sets. **Yield: 6 to 8 servings.**

NEW SOUTH STRING BEANS

1 cup pecans, coarsely chopped
¾ cup extra virgin olive oil
¼ cup white wine vinegar
1 tablespoon fresh, chopped rosemary
2 to 3 cloves garlic, minced
½ teaspoon salt
¼ teaspoon pepper
1½ pounds fresh string beans
1 small purple onion, thinly sliced
1 (4-ounce) package tomato-basil feta cheese, crumbled

Preheat oven to 350°. Place pecans in a single layer on a cookie sheet and toast for 5 to 8 minutes. Set aside. Combine oil, vinegar, rosemary, garlic, salt, and pepper in a large bowl. Set aside. Cut green beans into thirds and cook in boiling water until crisp-tender, about 20 minutes. Drain and rinse with cold water to stop cooking process. Spread on paper towels to absorb excess water. Add beans, pecans, onion, and cheese to the large bowl and toss with vinaigrette. Cover and chill. **Yield: 8 servings.**

SUNDAY SQUASH

3 pounds yellow squash
~ salt and pepper to taste
1 small onion, chopped
1 small green bell pepper, chopped

1 cup grated Parmesan cheese
1 cup mayonnaise
2 eggs, beaten

Slice squash into 1/2-inch rounds and cook in water seasoned with salt and pepper until tender, approximately 15

minutes. Drain. Combine remaining ingredients and add to squash. Pour into a greased 8 1/2 x 11 x 2-inch casserole. Bake at 350° for 40 minutes. **Yield: 8 to 10 servings.**

COCONUT CAKE WITH PINEAPPLE FILLING

1 cup sugar
1/2 cup butter
2 cups all-purpose flour
1 cup milk
3 egg whites, beaten with 1/4 cup sugar
2 1/2 teaspoons baking powder
1/4 teaspoon salt
1 teaspoon vanilla
~ Pineapple Filling
~ Seven-Minute Frosting
1 1/2 to 2 cups flaked coconut, fresh or frozen

Cream sugar and butter. Add flour alternating with milk. Fold in beaten egg whites. Add baking powder, salt, and vanilla and continue beating. Pour into 3 greased and floured 8-inch cake pans. Bake at 350° for 20 to 25 minutes or until toothpick inserted in center comes out clean. Cool on racks. To assemble, spread Pineapple Filling between layers. Frost top and sides of cake with Seven-Minute Frosting. Sprinkle coconut over sides and top of cake. Cover and store in refrigerator.

PINEAPPLE FILLING:

1 (15 1/4-ounce) can of crushed pineapple, well drained
1 or 2 egg yolks
1 heaping teaspoon cornstarch
1/2 cup sugar

Mix all ingredients in the top of a double boiler. Cook over boiling water until mixture thickens like a custard. Set aside to cool.

SEVEN-MINUTE FROSTING:

2 egg whites
1 1/2 cups sugar
5 tablespoons water
1 1/2 teaspoons light corn syrup
1 teaspoon vanilla

Combine egg whites, sugar, water, and corn syrup in top of double boiler, beating with hand mixer until thoroughly mixed. Cook over rapidly boiling water, beating constantly. Cook 7 minutes or until frosting will stand in peaks. Remove from heat. Add vanilla and beat until thick enough to spread.

OPPOSITE, TOP: **New South String Beans** in antique Haviland and Company Limoges china. OPPOSITE, BOTTOM: **Sunday Dinner.** Sterling flatware is **Francis I.** TOP: **Coconut Cake.** BOTTOM: **Dogwood tree in bloom.**

Mary McKay was a Vicksburg institution. She was feisty, smart, crafty, assertive, effusive, aggressive, talkative, and sometimes downright obnoxious – whatever it took to establish her Old Southern Tea Room as one of the South's finest eating places. She succeeded, too. Vicksburgers and visitors alike raved about the food, the American Automobile Association gave the Tea Room a top AAA rating, and Duncan Hinds himself graciously offered his "Duncan Hinds Approved" blessing. You knew you had dined well when you left the Old Southern Tea Room. It opened as a joint six-week gesture of "society" women in 1941 to introduce tourists to Southern cooking. But the determined Mrs. McKay decided it should stay open longer. She borrowed $100, bought a $7.50 stove without an oven door, and the Tea Room stayed open until 1987, when it closed following a fire. Elvira Coleman, who started out as Mrs. McKay's domestic help, was the original cook. Her assistant's main job was to hold fast an oven door for the $7.50 stove so her biscuits wouldn't fall. These small, round delights with flaky tops and buttery taste became almost as famous as the restaurant was for its traditional fare and genteel ambiance. Here was a dining style reminiscent of the best of plantation life.

Laurin Fields Stamm

One Sunday morning a friend and I ate breakfast at the Old Southern Tea Room. Seated at a table next to us was a man who clearly had experienced too much vacation. He was a big man, irritable and intimidating. His wife and children quietly watched as he fumed and fussed. Finally, breakfast arrived at their table. He inquired as to the white stuff on his plate. The waitress explained, "Grits, Sir." He didn't order grits and he wasn't going to pay for them. The waitress sweetly said that was fine. He boomed that she didn't understand. He didn't order grits and he didn't want them on his plate. The waitress explained to him that at the Old Southern Tea Room no one ordered grits – "They just come" – and she flatly refused to take them off his plate.

Rigby Maupin

Cameron Place

Annabelle

The mannered, Victorian, brick house called Annabelle was yet another of the houses built by the rich and munificent John Alexander Klein in the mid-19th century. This one was built for his son Madison in or about 1868 and faces what was once the old Marine Hospital.

Annabelle was, and is, a spacious and commodious family town house rather than a grand mansion. In the earlier decades of our present century, it was right in the middle of a thriving, vibrant neighborhood that spanned Oak Street to the north and extended to Klein Street on the south side, embracing Pearl Street, which runs parallel to the Mississippi River.

"I grew up in that house," says Vicksburg architect S. J. Tuminello about Annabelle, "and my cousin lived up in Cedar Grove. Back then, the neighborhood was wonderful – many first-generation European immigrants lived around here, and everything was beautifully kept.

"Then the railroad just more or less stole the right-of-way and tore down so many fine houses. The old Porterfield mansion is gone – and then, of course, Urban Renewal came along in the sixties and another six or seven fine old places were destroyed. It was such a crime."

Tuminello, who has been a key player in the authentic restorations and vernacular-style new constructions around town, is gratified to note the new spirit of preservationism that has taken hold, particularly in his childhood neighborhood.

Annabelle was bought a few years ago by Carol and George Mayer and put on public display as a gracious example of life in the area before the train tracks cut through the neighborhood. Himself a European of Czech birth, Mayer and his wife have meticulously refurbished Annabelle and its terrace and garden. Overnight guests can stroll the old brick streets, dine up the hill at Cedar Grove, and sniff the heady river air that hasn't changed much over the decades.

"The house has remained very much as I remember it as a boy," notes Tuminello. "The Mayers subdivided the two huge bathrooms for their guests' convenience, but the rooms look very much as they did."

The Mayers have many period pieces lovingly collected over the years, as well as some inherited treasures. But the dining room is furnished just as it was originally – the table and chairs were placed there in 1868.

Time and the heedless hand of man may have brought down many neighboring houses in this venerable district by the river, but Annabelle still sits comfortably among several old friends.

Brenda Ware Jones

RIVERFEST KICKOFF DINNER

Since Vicksburg's early days, the waterfront has been the source of freewheeling good times. Riverfest, an annual, three-day street party, is known for barrels of hot crawfish, cold beer, and enough fun activities to float anybody's boat – Mississippi Riverboat that is.

Sangria
Homemade Hot Tamales
Beef Shish Kabobs
Angel Hair Flans
Corn Salad with Cilantro Dressing
Strawberry Soufflé

SANGRIA

2	fifths California red Zinfandel
1 3/4	cups orange juice
1/3	cup lemon juice
1/4	cup sugar
1/4	cup brandy
1/3	cup orange-flavored liqueur
2	oranges, sliced
2	lemons, sliced
1 3/4	cups soda water
~	additional orange slices to garnish

Mix wine, orange juice, lemon juice, sugar, brandy, orange-flavored liqueur, orange slices, and lemon slices. Refrigerate at least 2 hours before serving. Just before serving, add soda water. Garnish each glass with an orange slice. Yield: 16 to 20 servings.

ABOVE: **Dinner on Haviland & Company china. Nineteenth-century Chippendale chair.** RIGHT: **Dining room.**

HOMEMADE HOT TAMALES

Tamale Filling:

- 2   medium to large onions
- 3   cloves garlic
- 2   pounds ground beef
- 2   tablespoons salt
- 1   teaspoon red pepper
- ½   cup regular cornmeal, white or yellow
- ½   cup water
- 1   cup tomato sauce
- 3   tablespoons chili powder
- 1   teaspoon cumin

In food processor fitted with metal blade, chop onions and garlic until puréed. In a large bowl, combine ground beef and remaining ingredients. Add onion and garlic and mix thoroughly.

Tamales:

- 2   cups cornmeal
- 1   teaspoon red pepper
- 1   (8-ounce) bag corn shucks
- ~   Tamale Filling
- 2   cups water
- 1   (46-ounce) can seasoned tomato juice
- 2   tablespoons chili powder

Combine cornmeal and red pepper in a 9 x 13 x 2-inch pan. Soak corn shucks in hot water. Unroll shucks into individual shucks and rinse thoroughly. Keep wet until ready to use, draining just a few at a time. To assemble, take one heaping tablespoon of tamale filling and form into a cigar shape. Roll in cornmeal. Place tamale filling in a corn shuck and roll up. Tear strips from another corn shuck to make ties and tie off each end of the tamale. Continue until tamale filling is used. In a large stockpot, layer tamales, alternating direction of the layers. Pour in 2 cups water, tomato juice, and chili powder. Put a plate on top of tamales to weight them down and put lid on pot. Bring to a boil, reduce heat, and simmer 1 hour. Untie, unroll, and enjoy! Tamales can be refrigerated and reheated in juices over low heat. **Yield: 6 dozen.**

BEEF SHISH KABOB

- ½   cup soy sauce
- 3   tablespoons honey
- 2   tablespoons vinegar
- 1½   teaspoons garlic powder
- 1½   teaspoons ginger
- ¾   cup oil
- 1   green onion, chopped
- 2½   pounds boneless-beef top sirloin, cut into 1½-inch cubes
- 1   pound low-fat Polish sausage, sliced into rounds
- 1   (8-ounce) can pineapple chunks, drained
- 3   green bell peppers, seeded and cut into 1½-inch pieces
- 2   red onions, cut into 1½-inch wedges
- 10   (8-inch) metal skewers

Mix soy sauce, honey, vinegar, garlic powder, ginger, oil, and green onion. Add sirloin and marinate several hours or overnight. Drain meat. Skewer beef, sausage, pineapple, and vegetables in desired pattern. Grill over hot coals for 18 to 20 minutes. **Yield: 10 servings.**

LEFT: **Homemade Hot Tamales served on hand-painted Victorian fish plates. Rug is antique Persian.**

ANGEL HAIR FLANS

1   cup whipping cream
3   large eggs
1   teaspoon minced fresh thyme or 1 pinch dried
½   teaspoon ground nutmeg
~   salt and pepper
1   cup freshly-grated Parmesan cheese, divided
3   ounces angel hair pasta, cooked al dente

Preheat oven to 350°. Grease 8 one-half-cup soufflé dishes or ramekins. Whisk whipping cream, eggs, thyme, and nutmeg in a medium bowl to blend. Season generously with salt and pepper. Stir in 2/3 cup Parmesan cheese. Divide pasta evenly among the dishes. Pour egg mixture over pasta, dividing equally among the dishes. Sprinkle flans with the remaining Parmesan cheese. Bake until flans are set and golden brown, about 20 minutes. Run small, sharp knife around sides of dishes to loosen. Unmold and serve. **Yield: 8 servings.**

CORN SALAD WITH CILANTRO DRESSING

2   bunches fresh cilantro, stemmed (about 2½ cups)
¾   cup oil
⅓   cup white wine vinegar
1½ tablespoons fresh lime juice
½   jalapeno pepper, chopped
½   shallot
½   teaspoon salt
9   ears fresh corn or 1 pound bag of frozen corn
¼   cup corn oil
1   small onion, finely chopped
½   tablespoon peeled, fresh ginger, finely chopped
1   red bell pepper, diced
1   green bell pepper, diced

Combine cilantro, oil, vinegar, lime juice, jalapeno, shallot, and salt in blender and purée. Set aside. Boil corn until tender, about 8 minutes. Cool. Cut corn off cob. If using frozen corn, cook according to package directions and cool. Heat corn oil and sauté onion until translucent, about 10 minutes. Add ginger and bell peppers and sauté for 5 minutes. Add corn and sauté until heated through. Transfer corn mixture to a large bowl. Pour dressing over and toss. Cover and refrigerate until cold. Can be made a day ahead. **Yield: 10 servings.**

⬛

TOP LEFT: Gentlemen's Cockfighting Chair from William and Mary period. RIGHT TOP: Strawberry Soufflé on Royal Doulton china. Sterling fork is Baltimore Rose by Kirk. BOTTOM LEFT: English piano desk, circa 1850, in the parlour. BOTTOM RIGHT: Garden bench on the front porch.

STRAWBERRY SOUFFLÉ

½   cup pecans, coarsely chopped
1   cup flour
⅓   cup brown sugar
½   cup butter, melted
4   egg whites
½   cup sugar
3   tablespoons lemon juice
3   tablespoons orange-flavored liqueur
2   (10-ounce) packages frozen sliced strawberries, thawed
1   (12-ounce) carton frozen whipped topping

Mix pecans, flour, sugar, and butter to make crumb mixture. Spread into a 9 x 13 x 2-inch pan and bake at 350° for 20 minutes, stirring often. Remove from oven and let cool. Remove 1/3 of crumbs and reserve for topping. Spread remaining crumbs evenly over bottom of pan. Beat egg whites until peaks form. Slowly add sugar and beat 5 more minutes. Fold in lemon juice, liqueur, and drained strawberries. Fold in whipped topping. Spread mixture over crumbs. Sprinkle reserved crumbs on top. Cover and freeze for at least 6 hours. Remove and let stand at room temperature for 20 minutes before serving. Cut into squares. Serves 12 to 16.

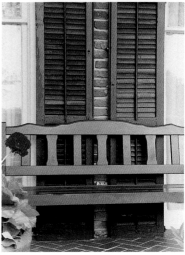

Annabelle

Loosa Yokena Plantation

Loosa Yokena Plantation is, as the country folks say, down the road a piece. Turn off Highway 61 South onto Jeff Davis Road, wind around a deeply shaded curve or two, and before you know it, you are about as deep into Warren County history as you can get.

Loosa Yokena took its name from the last chief of the Choctaw Indian tribe. The farm, which at one point in the early nineteenth century amounted to some 8,000 acres of cotton, has been in operation longer than the state of Mississippi – since the 1790s. Even more remarkable, it has remained in the possession of the same family for those 200 years. John Leigh Hyland, who with his wife Dee lives on the place, is the latest in a long, long line of Hylands to farm the land.

The first was James Hyland. He was an English Tory who acquired a land grant from the Spanish government, which in 1797 owned the territory.

In 1838, William Lewis Sharkey married into the Hyland family. He was Mississippi's first Supreme Court justice, then a member of the legislature in 1829, and after the Civil War a provisional governor. An interesting aside about Sharkey, he wrote the law in the 1830s granting women the right to retain sole title to property after marriage, rather than having it become the husband's possession. Sharkey's bill made Mississippi the first state to give women this right.

In 1860, John Gould and Patty Hyland Gould bought the plantation from the Sharkeys. When Gould died in 1878, his widow Patty continued to live on the place. She later remarried, and she and her second husband, Will Hankinson, built the present house in 1896. The architect was William Stanton, best known for designing Stanton Hall in Natchez. A large, rambling, late-Victorian, clapboard structure, the Hyland house retains the *de rigueur* wide central hallway of older vernacular houses. A deep wraparound porch was added at a later date.

The original 8,000 acres remained intact until 1927, when Patty Hyland Gould Hankinson died and the estate was divided among the heirs. Today, the Hylands own some 2,000 acres; much of it John Leigh plants in soybeans, which replaced cotton as the cash crop in the latter part of this century.

Dee, an enthusiastic gardener, has herb beds, perennials, annuals galore, and, most recently, an all-white garden inspired by Sissinghurst in England. All this is in addition to the generations-old bulbs that still pop up each spring and camellias and crepe myrtles that were planted before the turn of the century.

Mississippians have always cherished close ties with the earth, the owners of Loosa Yokena more so than most, perhaps. A lot of family stories can accumulate in two hundred years.

Brenda Ware Jones

AN EVENING IN THE COUNTRY

An invitation to the country is an invitation to slow down. If you don't make the transition easily, the cattle gap will begin to do it for you. The sights and sounds are so . . . yes, country – the pop of the screen door, a stroll through the white garden, acres and acres stretched out before you, and the casual elegance of entertaining al fresco.

Smooth Pineapple Daiquiris

Campbell's Swamp Shrimp

Easy Stuffed Mushrooms

Artichoke and Red Pepper Pizza

Penne with Crawfish and Sun-Dried Tomatoes

Yokena Cherry Pudding

LEFT: **Dinner seen through the all-white garden.**
ABOVE: **Easy Stuffed Mushrooms on Annie Glass in a bed of sage.**

SMOOTH PINEAPPLE DAIQUIRIS

1   (6-ounce) can frozen
    limeade
6   ounces light rum
8   slices of canned pineapple
2/3 cup vanilla ice cream
~   ice

Combine limeade and rum in a blender.
Add pineapple and ice cream. Blend
well. With the blender running, add a
few pieces of ice. Continue adding ice
until the mixture is smooth and thick
and the blender is nearly full. **Yield:** 4
servings.

CAMPBELL'S SWAMP SHRIMP

1   pound medium headless
    shrimp, unpeeled
1   tablespoon olive oil
1/2 cup Worcestershire sauce
1/4 cup bottled Italian dressing
2   lemons
~   seasoned salt
~   cracked black pepper
4   tablespoons margarine

Wash shrimp. Coat bottom of a 9 x 13 x
2-inch pan with olive oil. Place shrimp
in the pan side by side. Do not overlap.
Pour the Worcestershire sauce and
Italian dressing over shrimp. Squeeze
lemons over shrimp. Sprinkle shrimp
lightly with seasoned salt and heavily
with black pepper. Slice margarine very
thin and distribute over shrimp. Broil 18
to 20 minutes. Serve with French bread.
The shrimp are meant to be eaten with
the shells intact.

EASY STUFFED MUSHROOMS

1   pound fresh, medium-sized
    mushrooms
1/2 pound hot sausage
1/8 to 1/4 cup Parmesan cheese

Wipe and remove stems from
mushrooms. Form sausage balls, using
1 to 1 1/2 teaspoons sausage, and place
in each mushroom. Sprinkle each with
Parmesan cheese. Place stuffed
mushrooms in a lightly- greased 9 x 13
x 2-inch baking dish. Bake at 350° for
25 to 30 minutes. Serve immediately.

SPRING IN THE DEEP SOUTH

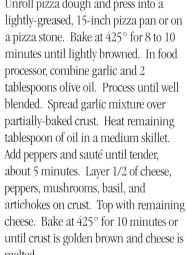

ARTICHOKE AND RED PEPPER PIZZA

1   (10-ounce) can
    refrigerated pizza crust

4   cloves garlic

3   tablespoons olive oil,
    divided

2   red bell peppers, cut into
    1/4-inch strips

1   (12-ounce) package
    shredded mozzarella
    cheese, divided

1   (4.5-ounce) jar sliced
    mushrooms

1   teaspoon dried basil

1   (6.5-ounce) jar marinated
    artichokes, drained and
    chopped

Unroll pizza dough and press into a lightly-greased, 15-inch pizza pan or on a pizza stone. Bake at 425° for 8 to 10 minutes until lightly browned. In food processor, combine garlic and 2 tablespoons olive oil. Process until well blended. Spread garlic mixture over partially-baked crust. Heat remaining tablespoon of oil in a medium skillet. Add peppers and sauté until tender, about 5 minutes. Layer 1/2 of cheese, peppers, mushrooms, basil, and artichokes on crust. Top with remaining cheese. Bake at 425° for 10 minutes or until crust is golden brown and cheese is melted.

OPPOSITE, TOP: Late-1700s log house.
OPPOSITE, BOTTOM: Wisteria.
OPPOSITE, LEFT: Campbell's Swamp Shrimp on Annie Glass in the herb garden.

TOP LEFT: Artichoke and Red Pepper Pizza. TOP, MIDDLE: Spanish moss dripping from the trees. TOP, RIGHT: Cistern house. BOTTOM, LEFT: An old building and wisteria. BOTTOM, RIGHT: The front porch.

Loosa Yokena Plantation

PENNE WITH CRAWFISH AND SUN-DRIED TOMATOES

- 3 tablespoons olive oil
- 2 cloves garlic, minced
- 2 tablespoons fresh basil, chopped
- 8 ounces crawfish tails
- 1 (3-ounce) package dry-packed, sun-dried tomatoes
- 2 green onions, finely chopped
- 1/2 green bell pepper, julienned
- 1/2 red bell pepper, julienned
- 1 Roma tomato, chopped
- 1/4 cup white wine
- 1 cup heavy cream
- 1/2 cup freshly-grated Parmesan cheese
- 12 ounces penne pasta, cooked al dente
- ~ salt and cracked pepper to taste

Place sauté pan on high heat. Add olive oil. When oil is hot, add garlic, basil, crawfish, and sun-dried tomatoes. Stir until crawfish tails are cooked, about 7 to 8 minutes. Add the green onions, peppers, and Roma tomato. Cook for 2 minutes. Add white wine and deglaze pan. Add heavy cream and cook until thickened, about 3 to 5 minutes. Add cheese and stir. Toss in hot pasta; season with salt and pepper. **Yield: 6 servings.**

LEFT: Penne with Crawfish and Sun-Dried Tomatoes on Concorde by Haviland & Company. Sterling silver flatware is antique Louis XV by Whiting, now a division of Gorham. Old family crystal. TOP: Dinner on the grounds. RIGHT: The front entrance.

YOKENA CHERRY PUDDING

2 cups unsweetened pie cherries, drained (reserve juice)
1¼ cups sugar
1 cup flour
½ cup pecans, chopped
1 teaspoon cinnamon
1 teaspoon baking soda
¼ teaspoon salt
1 egg, beaten
1 tablespoon butter, melted
~ Cherry Sauce
~ Sweetened Whipped Cream

Combine all ingredients except Cherry Sauce and Sweetened Whipped Cream and beat until well blended. Pour into a greased 8-inch square pan. Bake at 325° for 40 minutes. Let cool. Refrigerate until ready to assemble individual desserts. Spoon Cherry Sauce onto dessert plate. Place a square of cherry pudding in sauce and top with Sweetened Whipped Cream. **Yield:** 8 to 10 servings.

CHERRY SAUCE:

1 cup reserved cherry juice, adding water to make 1 cup if necessary
½ cup sugar
1 tablespoon butter, melted
1 tablespoon cornstarch
2 drops red food coloring

Mix all ingredients in a small saucepan. Cook until thickened. Cool.

SWEETENED WHIPPED CREAM:

½ pint heavy cream
2 tablespoons powdered sugar

Beat cream with electric mixer until peaks begin to form. Add sugar and continue beating until stiff.

TOP: **Dessert in the foyer.**
BOTTOM: **Yokena Cherry Pudding.**

THE COON DOG EULOGY

Let not your hearts be troubled for in his master's swamp are many den trees. If it were not so, I would have told you.

He has gone to prepare a place for you and where he shall go, Ole Red will go also.

Dogs, they say, do not have souls; they only have hide and bones. But I believe there is a coon dog heaven, and Ole Red is gone where the good coon dogs go.

Anybody that coon hunts has to believe in God. If you have known the music of coon hounds on a trail and heard the excitement in their voices when they tree; if you have seen their courage and bravery in a tough fight with an old boar coon; if you have heard their anguished cries and howls; if you have seen the ugly gashes and bleeding wounds and witnessed their resolve to never quit; you know there has to be a God to make an animal like that. A God that would make a coon dog won't forget him when he is gone. There is a coon dog heaven. And Ole Red is there.

And every night he runs and the den trees are there in the old swamp. And the old hunter's moon hangs low in the west and the coons don't go up slick bark trees and the carbide don't run out and there ain't no bull beetle and saw briars. And Old Master always knocks the coon out and lets Ole Red grab him and give him a good shake; and then he gets a pat on the head and climbs back in the kennel in back of the pick-up and goes home and sleeps all day. 'Cause he knows in coon dog heaven, he can hunt again when the sun goes down and the tree frogs holler.

May the bones of Ole Red rest in peace, through the mercy of God, and may the coon hunters' light perpetually shine upon him. Amen.

Eulogy written and delivered by Bill Ramsey, Vicksburg attorney, at the funeral of a Vicksburg coon dog held at the National Coon Dog Cemetery in Red Bay, Alabama, in 1977. The funeral was attended by approximately 30 coon hunters from Vicksburg, local Alabama hunters with their dogs, and The Associated Press.

Loosa Yokena Plantation

Belle of the Bends

Belle of the Bends used to be a boat but is now a house. No, it wasn't dry docked and converted – they're two completely different structures, actually. It was strictly a nomenclature trick. You see, the original *Belle of the Bends* was a steamboat piloted by Captain Tom Morrissey, who was the grandfather of the present Belle (house, not boat) owner, Josephine Pratt. He never lived in this house – in fact, we all knew it growing up as the "Buelow house." Captain Morrissey lived in the "Morrissey house," now rechristened Cameron Place, up by the jailhouse. Are you confused yet? If so, you must not be from here – or from the South for that matter. This sort of serpentine narrative makes perfect sense to us.

And living in this Victorian Italianate-style house on Klein Street makes perfect sense to Wallace and Josephine Pratt, who bought it in 1990 and restored it into an exquisite bed and breakfast. Her blood connection to the river is reconfirmed each time she looks out one of the bedroom windows or stands on the wraparound verandas. From here, the marshlands of Louisiana are visible over that swath of slow-moving, brown water that is the Mississippi River.

The house was built in 1876 by Mississippi Senator Murray F. Smith and his wife Kate. Long central hallways, designed to catch the river breezes in those days before electrically-controlled climates, run front to back in both stories. The era was a voluptuous one architecturally; after a hard decade of Reconstruction and rebuilding, those who could afford to caught the spirit of Victorian excess. Senator and Mrs. Smith chose lavish appointments like the bronze and frosted-glass gasoliers original to the house and still glowing in the main parlor and dining room. Skilled craftsmen were engaged to produce the intriguing oval-arched woodwork over the doorways, a romantic departure from the pedimented and Greek-key styles of the pre-War era.

Many of the furnishings in the house have remained for over 100 years – in true Southern style, things just got left where they were first placed and were sold as part of the real estate. Perhaps this gives the Belle of the Bends its sense of timeless rightness, as though an intervening century has not passed.

The original stables and separate cooking quarters were destroyed many years ago and were replaced by contemporary parking and a much more convenient in-house kitchen. But much else remains just as it looked when the Senator and his wife entertained guests there. Jo and Wally Pratt have added lush period landscaping, including a rose garden, for guests' enjoyment on crisp, spring evenings.

Lounging against the upstairs porch balustrade, squinting to figure out where the Mississippi and the Yazoo Rivers join, you might think you are on a riverboat somewhere between Memphis and New Orleans.

That's the idea behind Belle of the Bends – the house, that is.

Brenda Ware Jones

DESSERT AFTER
GOLD IN THE HILLS

Back in 1936 Julia Arnold wanted to stage a melodrama for the tourists. Pilgrimage officials laughed and instead decided on a History of Vicksburg pageant. Opening night, rain left the outdoor stage a muddy mess and some of the actors, "both Indians and palefaces, had too much firewater." So, Gold in the Hills won out after all and has never stopped. Listed in the Guinness Book of World Records as the longest-running melodrama, Gold audiences throw peanuts and hiss the villain, call out pleas and advice to Little Nell, sing with the waiters, and everyone, including pilgrimage officials, laughs.

Tiramisu Cake with Chocolate Sauces

White Chocolate Sauce

Dark Chocolate Sauce

ABOVE: **Tiramisu Cake served on Empress Dresden Flowers china by Schumann.**

43

TIRAMISU CAKE

- ~ butter recipe cake mix
- 6 egg yolks
- 1¼ cups sugar
- 2 (8-ounce) packages cream cheese
- 1 pint heavy cream, whipped
- 3 ounces Kahlúa
- ½ cup espresso or strong-brewed coffee
- ~ cocoa
- ~ confectioners' sugar
- ~ White Chocolate Sauce
- ~ Dark Chocolate Sauce

Prepare cake mix according to package directions and bake in 2 round layers. When cake has cooled, slice each layer to make four layers. Place waxed paper between layers and refrigerate until ready to assemble cake. Beat together egg yolks and sugar in top of double boiler until smooth and lemon colored. Bring water to a boil, reduce heat to low, and cook 10 minutes, stirring constantly. Remove mixture from heat. Stir in cream cheese, beating well. Let cool to room temperature. Fold cream cheese mixture into whipped cream. Refrigerate for 1 hour. Combine Kahlúa and espresso. To assemble cake, place first layer on cake plate and brush with Kahlúa mixture. Spread cream cheese mixture until barely spills over the edge. Repeat with remaining cake layers, finishing with cream cheese mixture. Dust top of cake with cocoa and confectioners' sugar. Serve with White Chocolate Sauce and Dark Chocolate Sauce swirled together on plate.

TOP: Tiramisu Cake on piano.
BOTTOM: *Belle of the Bends* docked at Vicksburg waterfront about 1900. Photograph by J. Mack Moore. OPPOSITE, RIGHT: Detail of Dresden compote.

WHITE CHOCOLATE SAUCE

4   ounces white chocolate
3/4 cup heavy cream

Melt white chocolate. Heat cream to boiling point. Whisk cream into melted chocolate until smooth. Refrigerate until ready to use.

DARK CHOCOLATE SAUCE

1   cup half & half
1/2 cup sugar
1/4 cup cocoa
3   tablespoons butter
1   teaspoon vanilla extract

Combine half & half, sugar, cocoa, and butter in heavy, small saucepan. Whisk over low heat until sugar dissolves and butter melts. Increase heat to medium and whisk until sauce just begins to simmer. Remove from heat. Stir in vanilla. Cool before serving.

Gold in the Hills traveled to Pittsburgh in 1956 and I went along with the cast and crew as Mayor of Vicksburg. When we docked, Pittsburgh's mayor met us, opened his arms, gave us the key to the city, and told me that if there was anything we wanted, just to ask for it. At the first night's performance we all had a ball – the audience was throwing peanuts, booing, and hissing – just a great time. But when it was time to leave, we realized we had a problem. It was pouring down rain and we had no transportation. We stood around a while wondering what to do when I spotted the perfect solution, a paddy wagon. I went up the driver, told him who I was, and explained that Mayor Morris told us we could have anything in Pittsburgh we wanted. He loaded us all up. What a sight we were, especially when we arrived at our elegant hotel!

John D. Holland

I played the villain in Gold in the Hills *for thirty-five years and most of my friends say that imminently qualified me for my daytime job as a mortgage banker, but that is another story ... Most of the additions to* Gold in the Hills *were advertently or inadvertently written into, and became a part of, this classic show. For example, in the third act when Nellie returns home from the city, there is a storm outside with snow falling heavily. The stagehand opened the door for Nellie to enter the stage, but neglected the snow that should have followed her. Julia Arnold, the director, came from the other side of the stage, whispering in a loud voice, "The snow, the snow!" The stagehand immediately cracked the door slightly and threw the snow in, exposing his hand and his arm. The reaction was astounding – the crowd cheered and applauded. The heroine could not understand what she had done to get such a reception. Needless to say, we had another well-received part added to the show.*

Shouphie Habeeb

Belle of the Bends

AMBROSIA

SUMMER IN THE DEEP SOUTH

Mississippi summers are simply
hot and humid.
Nothing else.
And nothing else matters.

The things that define the Deep South
are products of the summer climate.
Seersucker suits,
white dresses,
barefoot children,
ceiling fans,
long, slow drawls.
Mint juleps,
porch swings,
mimosa blossoms,
straw hats, and
gentle men.

Some think the heat is stifling.
Vicksburgers think it is an opportunity
to slow down life's pace
and enjoy.

Martha Hickman Day

Martha Hickman Day, a native of North Carolina, has lived in Vicksburg since 1962. She was society editor for The Vicksburg Post *from 1971 until 1992. She served as president of the Junior Auxiliary of Vicksburg from 1973 to 1974.*

Grey Oaks Estates

If you expect to see Miss Scarlett gracefully wind her way around the stately columns of Grey Oaks, you might not be too disappointed.

Grey Oaks is the only still-standing replica of Tara, the mansion in Margaret Mitchell's Civil War epic, *Gone With the Wind*.

Now owned by Dr. and Mrs. Donald Street Hall, the home is an elegant adaptation of an 1830s home. Surrounded by six acres of magnificently landscaped gardens, towering oaks, and mountains of kudzu, the house takes on the aura of a romance novel.

Mrs. Hall enjoys talking about the home she and her husband share with their daughter, Katherine.

"We have here in Grey Oaks the best of both worlds," she said. "The history is unique."

Originally built on the outskirts of Port Gibson in Greek Revival style, the house was once called Anchuka. It was bought in 1940 by Michael Morrissey of Vicksburg. No record exists of the purchase price.

Under the supervision of architect James T. Canizaro of Jackson, Mississippi, the house was dismantled and all salvageable parts were used to rebuild the home in Vicksburg. The newly-built house was redesigned in the Federal style and renamed Grey Oaks.

On the beautiful circular drive to the mansion, guests may stroll among the giant oaks from which Grey Oaks takes its name. And in the spring, Grey Oaks takes on a rainbow of colors with its blooming dogwoods, azaleas, forsythia, spiraea, and flowering bulbs. The nature trails through the woods invite guests to enjoy Mississippi's native woodlands of greenery and birds.

An avid antique collector, Mrs. Hall has always loved meeting people.

"I've had so much fun with this house," she said. "Katherine was just five months old when we moved here. Don and I looked at many houses in the area, but when we saw Grey Oaks, we knew this would be more than a house for us. It would be a home."

At Grey Oaks, the Halls have made interior changes – adding rooms and closets, enlarging baths, and digging out the basement.

"We think the house is beautiful with exquisite milled woodwork, sterling silver doorknobs, French bronze chandeliers, and heart-of-pine sub-flooring with quarter-sewn oak on top," Hall said. The home is filled with 18th- and 19th-century period antiques, fine objects d'art, and antique oriental rugs.

The mood of Tara – rustling hoop skirts, candlelight, and gracious entertaining – sets the scene at sunset at beautiful Grey Oaks, just a stone's throw from the Mighty Mississippi River.   *Martha Hickman Day*

A Morning of Bridge

Bridge is a Southern ladies' institution. There are bridge clubs that are deadly serious with little or no conversation and immensely enjoyed by expert players. Then there are bridge clubs that serve as a fine excuse to get away from it all, drink ladies' frozen drinks, enjoy a lovely luncheon, and – if time allows – play a hand or two of cards.

Fresh Blackberries
Spinach Braid
Dilled Vegetable Salad
Watermelon Sorbet
Cream Cheese Roll-ups

SPINACH BRAID

½   pound spicy Italian pork sausage

⅓   cup coarsely shredded carrots

¼   cup chopped onion

1   (8-ounce) container cream cheese with chives and onions

1   (10-ounce) package frozen chopped spinach, thawed and drained

⅓   cup chopped toasted pecans

¼   cup dry bread crumbs

1   (16-ounce) loaf frozen bread dough, thawed (white or whole wheat)

2   teaspoons melted margarine or butter

~   German-style mustard

In a 10-inch skillet cook sausage, carrots, and onion until sausage is brown and onions are tender. Remove from heat and drain fat. Blend in cream cheese. Stir in spinach, pecans, and bread crumbs. On a lightly floured surface, roll dough into a 12 x 9-inch rectangle. Carefully transfer to a greased baking sheet. Spread filling lengthwise in a 3-inch line down center to within 1 inch of ends. Make 3-inch cuts from edges toward center at 1-inch intervals. Moisten end of each strip. Alternately fold opposite strips at an angle across filling. Let rise in warm place to double, about 30 minutes. Bake at 350° for 25 to 30 minutes. Brush top with melted margarine or butter. Serve with German-style mustard if desired. **Makes 10 to 12 servings.**

RIGHT: Antique country French game table of chestnut and yew wood, circa 1850, set with antique English majolica plates, European monogrammed crystal wine goblets and Mackenzie-Childs water goblets. Arrangement of wild hydrangeas, daylilies, and other summer blooms in an antique French jardinière.

49

DILLED VEGETABLE SALAD

1 large head of broccoli, separated into flowerets

1 head of cauliflower, separated into flowerets

4 carrots, sliced in rounds

1 red bell pepper, chopped into 1/2-inch pieces

1 cucumber, sliced in rounds

1 (8-ounce) can pitted whole black olives, drained

1/2 pound small fresh mushrooms or large ones, cut bite size

1 cup salad vinegar

1 tablespoon sugar

1 tablespoon dill weed

1 tablespoon garlic salt

1 teaspoon pepper

1 teaspoon salt

1 1/2 cups vegetable oil

Combine all vegetables in a large bowl. Mix vinegar, sugar, dill weed, garlic salt, pepper, salt, and oil. Pour over vegetables. Refrigerate overnight. Drain and serve on bed of lettuce for a salad or use as finger food for picnics or parties.

TOP, LEFT: **Spinach Braid and Dilled Vegetable Salad.**
TOP, RIGHT: **Watermelon Sorbet on Coalport plates.**
RIGHT: **Special collector's Dresden edition of Napoleon and his generals.**

SUMMER IN THE DEEP SOUTH

WATERMELON SORBET

2 cups water

1 cup sugar

4 cups peeled, diced, and seeded watermelon

1 (6-ounce) can frozen pink lemonade

~ cubes of watermelon and mint to garnish

Cook water and sugar over high heat until mixture just starts to boil. Cool. Purée watermelon in blender and push through a sieve. Add pink lemonade and sugar syrup to the sieved watermelon. Stir until well blended. Pour into container of electric ice cream freezer and freeze according to manufacturer's instructions. Spoon into glasses and top with cubes of chilled watermelon and a sprig of mint.

CREAM CHEESE ROLL-UPS

12 ounces cream cheese, softened
1/2 cup sugar
1 teaspoon almond extract
1 egg
2 loaves white sandwich bread
3/4 cup butter, melted
3/4 cup sugar

Beat together cream cheese, 1/2 cup sugar, almond extract, and egg. Trim crusts off bread and flatten each piece with a rolling pin. Keep bread slices under a damp paper towel so they do not dry out. Spread cream cheese mixture on bread slices and roll up jelly-roll fashion. Dip each roll in melted butter and roll in remaining sugar. Bake at 400° for 15 minutes. May be served warm or at room temperature. Rolls may be frozen before being dipped in butter and rolled in sugar. Makes approximately 30 rolls.

TOP: **Chandelier designed to hold a flower arrangement.**

The RTBC

It was considered vogue in the late 1960s for women to major in education. The formula was so simple. Get a degree. Get married. Teach school. Have a baby. Retire. Thus was the beginning of the RTBC – Retired Teachers' Bridge Club – established on Chambers Street in 1974.

For years the RTBC met every first and third Wednesday. Nobody missed – ever. We even cooked. We scoured every cookbook in the South for new egg casserole recipes. Some members even shopped while on vacation. One was particularly proud of herself for bringing the recipe Colorado Strata back from Vail.

We don't cook much now since someone discovered "ordering in," and RTBC bridge has expanded to other areas of entertainment. One Valentine's Day we watched "An Affair to Remember" – (sniff). The favors were decorated boxes of tissues. The appearance of Vicksburg's Scarlett (Ann Hall) on The Oprah Winfrey Show gave us a perfect excuse to gather around the T.V. (in our pearls, of course) to eat chicken salad sandwiches and stuffed eggs and read from the "Southern Bell Primer." A particularly memorable event was the "Miss RTBC Pageant" that was held one spring in Pensacola. It was good that we were out of town for this. RTBC rule #1 is "What happens out of town, stays out of town!"

The highlight of the RTBC year is Christmas Bridge. When it's your turn to have Christmas Bridge, just about everybody knows. Mainly because if someone asks you to do anything, you can't. You have Christmas Bridge. You get the house painted because you have...Christmas Bridge. You buy Christmas china because you have...Christmas Bridge. You put your tree up in October because you have...Christmas Bridge.

There is nothing that has not been dreamed up, polished, or decorated for Christmas Bridge. Gail Pittman even designed a Christmas plate with our names glazed on the back for our 20th anniversary. Speaking of dreams, last December we did something we only had talked about for years. Nine RTBCers headed to New York City . . . for Christmas Bridge.

Penny Sanders Varner

Grey Oaks Estates

51

The Corners

It is only fitting that the warm and inviting home, The Corners, is today the setting for many weddings and gala bridal parties. It was built as a wedding gift.

Completed by John Klein in 1873, The Corners served as a wedding gift to his daughter, Susan, and her husband, Isaac Bonham. The house built for Susan Klein was certainly not the only construction project undertaken by her father. He had previously built his home, Cedar Grove, in 1840 and then built a home for each of his other four children

when they married. Of the five children's homes, The Corners, is the only one that remains.

Built to overlook the majestic Mississippi River, the home is presently a popular bed and breakfast inn. It boasts seventeen bedrooms, several suites, and guest rooms out back in what was once the kitchen. The kitchen, once heavily damaged by fire, has been refurbished.

In the main house, the downstairs area has also been redesigned as a guest area. Most recently, a large guest house has been built to match the design of the main house. Owners Bettye and Cliff Whitney are assisted by their daughter-in-law, Kilby, and son, Cliff III, who help cater.

Purchased by the Whitneys in 1986, The Corners offered Bettye Whitney a feeling of love at first sight. "The view of the river, the large rooms, the whistle of the boats, the whole thing," she said. "I felt like a child again. The house spoke to me."

Built after the Civil War, the house is not antebellum, which means "before the war." It is an Italianate raised cottage and reflects the Victorian period. The floor plan was based on that of Cedar Grove.

The pierced columns surrounding the front gallery are unique to Vicksburg. There are about sixty other houses in the city that have the hand-carved columns known in architectural circles as Vicksburg pierced columns.

Between 1919 and 1959 The Corners had eight different owners. In 1959, Dr. and Mrs. Robert Ivy bought the house, which they shared with their children for twenty-six years until the Whitneys purchased the house.

Today, Bettye Whitney still finds excitement in The Corners. Each room is special to the family; and they strive to pass this feeling on to their guests, many of whom have returned again and again for another stay at The Corners.

Martha Hickman Day

A Bridesmaids' Luncheon

The typical Southern bride will marry in her family church with an alarming percentage of her sorority sisters as attendants. She will wear her mother's dress, carry her grandmother's lace handkerchief, and ride from the church to a plantation reception in a vintage horse and buggy. All of those present will cherish the event as a time when they are reminded of their own heritage and the elegance of the Old South.

Cream of Carrot Soup
Chicken and Artichoke Salad
Summer Tomatoes on Pesto Toast
Summer Fruits and Berries with Southern Cream
Lemon Angel Pie

CREAM OF CARROT SOUP

4 tablespoons sweet butter
1 cup finely chopped yellow onion
2 pounds carrots, peeled and chopped
6 cups chicken stock
1/2 cup orange juice
1/4 teaspoon red pepper
1 teaspoon salt
1/2 teaspoon black pepper
2 to 3 tablespoons sherry to taste

Melt butter in soup pot. Add onion and sauté until tender, about 20 minutes. Add carrots and 4 cups chicken stock. Bring to a boil. Reduce heat, cover, and simmer until carrots are tender, about 30 minutes. Pour the soup through a strainer. Reserve liquid and return to soup pot. Transfer solids to the bowl of a food processor and process until smooth. Return purée to the pot and add orange juice, seasonings, and sherry. Add additional stock, up to 2 cups, until soup is the desired consistency. Simmer until heated through. Serve immediately.
Yield: 6 servings.

CHICKEN AND ARTICHOKE SALAD

6 chicken breasts, cooked, boned, and chopped
1 cup salad olives, drained
1 (14-ounce) can artichoke hearts, drained and sliced
1 medium red onion, sliced
1/4 large green bell pepper, chopped
1/2 cup celery, chopped
1/2 pound fresh mushrooms, sliced
1/2 cup ripe olives, sliced
1/4 cup vegetable oil
1/4 cup olive oil
1/4 cup balsamic vinegar
1 tablespoon lemon juice
~ salt and black pepper to taste
~ cayenne pepper to taste
~ curly leaf lettuce

Combine chicken, salad olives, artichokes, red onion, green pepper, celery, mushrooms, and ripe olives in large bowl. In small bowl combine vegetable oil, olive oil, balsamic vinegar, lemon juice, salt, and peppers. Whisk to combine. Pour over salad. Refrigerate overnight. Serve on curly lettuce leaves.

TOP, LEFT: **Entrance gate.**
ABOVE: **Oil painting of an Italian count who married a Vicksburg lady.**
BOTTOM: **Cream of Carrot Soup served in antique Bavarian china, Royal Bereuth. Silver flatware is antique Imperial Chrysanthemum by Gorham.**

SUMMER TOMATOES
on PESTO TOAST

1   baguette loaf
~   mayonnaise
~   Pesto
6   ripe Roma tomatoes
~   fresh parsley or fresh basil

Slice baguette into 1/4-inch slices. Lightly toast slices on both sides under oven broiler. Let cool. Spread each bread slice with mayonnaise and pesto. Top with a tomato slice. Garnish with a sprig of parsley or a small basil leaf.

PESTO:

1/4   pound ham
1 1/2   cups olive oil, divided
1/2   cup Parmesan cheese, grated
1/4   cup Romano cheese, grated
3   to 3 1/2 cups fresh basil leaves
1/4   cup spinach, boiled, squeezed dry, and chopped
2   tablespoons pecans
2   tablespoons pine nuts
3   cloves garlic
1/2   teaspoon salt
1/2   teaspoon ground pepper

Chop ham in a food processor, remove, and set aside. Pour 1/2 cup olive oil in food processor. Add the rest of the ingredients and process until mixture is finely ground. Add 1 cup olive oil and process until smooth. Add ham and process just to mix. May be frozen.

LEFT: **View of parlour from the back gallery.** TOP: **A cabbage cart.** RIGHT: **Detail in the dining room from a French chateau, 1750.** OPPOSITE PAGE: **Lunch on the front gallery.**

SUMMER FRUITS and
BERRIES with
SOUTHERN CREAM

2 1/4   cups half & half
1   tablespoon unflavored gelatin
1   cup sugar
16   ounces sour cream
1   teaspoon vanilla
~   summer fruits and berries

Mix half & half, gelatin, and sugar. Heat in a double boiler, stirring until gelatin is completely dissolved. Remove from heat and fold in sour cream and vanilla. Pour into a stainless steel bowl and chill in an ice bath until mixture thickens. Store in refrigerator. Serve a dollop on top of individual dishes of any combination of strawberries, raspberries, blueberries, bananas, and peaches.
Yield: 4 cups.

LEMON ANGEL PIE

4 egg whites
½ teaspoon cream of tartar
¼ teaspoon salt
1 teaspoon vanilla, divided
1½ cups sugar, divided
4 egg yolks
¼ cup lemon juice
2 tablespoons grated lemon rind
~ dash of salt
1 cup whipping cream
2 tablespoons powdered sugar, sifted

Make meringue of egg whites, cream of tartar, salt, and 1/2 teaspoon vanilla. Beat until stiff but not dry. Gradually add about 2/3 cup sugar, beating constantly. Fold in another 1/3 cup sugar. Heap in a well-buttered, 9-inch glass pie plate. Bake at 275° for 1 hour or until dry and firm to touch, but not brown. Let cool. Meringue will sink as it cools. Combine egg yolks, 1/2 cup sugar, lemon juice, lemon rind, and dash of salt in top of a double boiler. Cook, stirring constantly, until thick and smooth. Let cool and spread over center of meringue. Refrigerate for several hours or overnight. About 1 hour before serving, whip the cream. Fold in 2 tablespoons powdered sugar and 1/2 teaspoon vanilla. Spread over lemon filling and chill until ready to serve.

This is a true story about Miss Carolyn and me. Thirty-something years ago we were up at my deer camp for what we called "Ladies' Day." The ONLY time the ladies could come to the deer camp was the Saturday after Thanksgiving. So I invited Lady Carolyn. We were engaged to be wed. And my dear, wonderful, lovable cook, whose name was Ernestine Bailey, was there. She was a splendid person, very comical, very ostentatious. We were all gathered in the dining room, if you can call it that – it's a deer camp – for supper. (We didn't call it dinner; we called it supper.) There were about 25 or 30 hunters, and I believe Miss Carolyn was the only female; but there may have been a couple of others.

Ernestine said to me, "Mr. Bill, is Miss Carolyn your intended?" And I said, "Well, yes, she is." She said, "Uh, Huh. Now, look a'here, Mr. Bill, let me ask you something. How old is Miss Carolyn?" I said, "She's twenty years old." And Ernestine said, "Uh, Huh, Mr. Bill, how old are you?" I said, "Thirty-seven." And she said, "Hmmm, Hmmm, Hmmm." I said, "Now wait a minute, Ernestine, don't be starting that 'Hmmm, Hmmm, Hmmm.' I want you to know that I'm in my prime." Ernestine shook her head and said, "Ooh, Lord, Mr. Bill, what you gonna do when Miss Carolyn gets in her prime?"

Bill Ramsey

One day I went up to the Rivertown Club, and there at the end of the line stood club manager, Warren Asher. Warren looked kind of like a cross between a ripe tomato and Winston Churchill. He was standing there with his lip poked out as far as his stomach. I knew he and his wife Kate had been on a trip. I said, "How are you, Warren?" "All right," he sighed. I said, "Warren, you and Kate have a nice trip?" He said, "Yeah." I said, "Second honeymoon, huh?" And he said, "Yeah. Only this time, it was I who went into the bathroom and cried."

Dick Ferguson

The Corners

The Mississippi River

The River. It's why we're here. Or, as more poetically stated by Michael Robinson, Chief of Public Affairs of the Mississippi River Commission, "The river defines and is the lifeblood of Vicksburg."

Two hundred years ago, the Reverend Newit Vick bought 1,120 acres on the river for $2 an acre and set about planning a city. The location was chosen because of the river.

Waterways meant commerce and prosperity in the 1800s. Steamboats transported people, exported cotton, brought oysters from New Orleans, furniture from St. Louis, and millwork from Cincinnati. All good things came from the riverboats. And there were a lot of them. Three hundred fifty steamboats were operating on the Mississippi in 1830 and dozens docked in Vicksburg on any given day. The people who got off those boats – people from Ireland, England, France, Italy, Lebanon, and Germany – all got off here with their own rich, cultural backgrounds and made Vicksburg their home.

Then came Vicksburg's appointment with war. Vicksburg citizens really were not interested in fighting; this was a merchant community that voted against secession at the state convention in Jackson. But when President Lincoln sent his gunboats to bombard the city from the river and General Grant and General Sherman to blockade land routes with their soldiers, Vicksburg people were resilient, holding out as long as they could against this siege. Why did Mr. Lincoln want Vicksburg so badly? The river. All those riverboats carrying food and artillery among the Confederate States were stopped. Control of the river meant control of the South and victory for the Union. Lincoln called Vicksburg "the key." In his dispatch reporting the city's surrender, Grant said that the key had been put in Mr. Lincoln's pocket.

More people and more commerce came in the years after the war, as did a year every Southerner can tell you was eventful and why: 1927. It was the year of the big flood. It was the year that the river, which had been the highway for so much prosperity, became almost demonic.

As William Faulkner put it, "The river was now doing what it liked to do, had waited patiently to do, as a mule will work for you ten years for the privilege of kicking you once." Vicksburg, its bluffs high and dry, became host to boatload after boatload of refugees – 15,000 in all.

After flooding nearly as devastating as war, Congress assigned the Corps of Engineers to do what it could to predict and control the river. And the result was a powerful presence of engineers and scientists relocating to the city to be close to – and to respectfully watch and steer – the nation's mightiest stream.

Today the commerce continues. Approximately 520 million tons of commodities from fuel to food are transported on barges up and down the stream each year. And about 22,000 vehicles and about 500 train cars pass over it on the bridges at Vicksburg each day.

Now and then Vicksburg people join visitors who stop and really look at the river for a while. They share anew an appreciation of its power and its beauty. And if they think about it, they realize the river is why we're here.

Martha Hickman Day

PICNIC AT THE RIVERFRONT PARK

What better setting for a family reunion than alongside the Mighty Mississippi? The Vicksburg Homecoming Benevolent Club has hosted this gigantic reunion of African-American families since 1976. The weekend-long event includes various opportunities for socializing as well as a means for those who have left Vicksburg to assist children and the needy through a scholarship fund in the place they call "home."

Barbeque Chicken on the Grill

Homecoming Baked Beans

Yazoo Marinated Vegetables

Cypress House Cole Slaw

Black-Eyed Pea Cornbread

Sugar Crust Cake

Peach Ice Cream

BARBECUE CHICKEN ON THE GRILL

1 (5-ounce) bottle Worcestershire sauce
2 tablespoons cider vinegar
1/3 cup oil
1 (20-ounce) bottle ketchup
1/2 cup brown sugar
1 teaspoon chili powder
1 teaspoon Tabasco
4 cloves garlic, minced
~ chicken pieces or halves

Mix first three ingredients and baste meat when first put on grill. Add remaining ingredients to leftover mixture and mix well. When meat is done, dip in sauce, and put back on the grill for a few minutes. **Yield:** approximately 1 quart.

CLOCKWISE, FROM LEFT: Black-Eyed Pea Cornbread, Sugar Crust Cake, lemonade, fresh tomatoes and cucumbers, Homecoming Baked Beans, and The Very Best Salsa!

HOMECOMING BAKED BEANS

1 (40-ounce) can pork and beans
1 (16-ounce) can green lima beans, drained
1 (15-ounce) can kidney beans, drained
1 (15½-ounce) can pineapple chunks (drain and reserve juice)
¾ cup ketchup
⅓ cup brown sugar
1 tablespoon prepared Dijon-style mustard
2 tablespoons Worcestershire sauce
2 tablespoons lemon juice
5 slices bacon, cut in 1-inch pieces
1 medium onion, chopped
1 green bell pepper, chopped
⅓ cup pineapple juice, or more

In a 3-quart baking dish, mix all beans, pineapple, catsup, brown sugar, mustard, Worcestershire sauce, lemon juice, bacon, onion, bell pepper, and pineapple juice. Stir well. Add more pineapple juice for juicier beans. Bake uncovered at 300° for 3 hours. Can be cooked in a crock pot on low for 5 to 6 hours. **Serve 10 to 12.**

YAZOO MARINATED VEGETABLES

1 cup wine vinegar
½ cup olive oil
¾ cup sugar
1 (15-ounce) can French-style green beans
1 (15-ounce) can very small English peas
1½ cups chopped celery
1½ cups chopped green bell pepper
1 (4-ounce) jar pimiento strips
2 medium onions, quartered
1 cup julienne beets, well drained
½ cup chopped cabbage

For marinade, combine vinegar, oil, and sugar. Mix well. Combine green beans, peas, celery, bell pepper, pimiento, and onions in a large bowl. Place beets in a separate bowl. Divide the marinade between the two bowls. Cover and refrigerate overnight. Just before serving, combine bean mixture, beets, and cabbage. Toss to combine. Serve immediately. **Serves 12 to 14.**

CYPRESS HOUSE COLE SLAW

1 medium head of cabbage
3 or 4 carrots
½ green bell pepper
½ small onion
¼ cup salad vinegar
¼ cup brown sugar
¼ to ½ cup Miracle Whip

SALAD DRESSING:

1 tablespoon celery seed
1 teaspoon Tabasco
1 tablespoon sweet relish
~ salt to taste
~ black pepper to taste

Shred or chop cabbage, carrots, bell pepper, and onion in food processor. In a separate bowl mix vinegar and brown sugar. Add Miracle Whip and seasonings. Pour dressing over the vegetables and stir until well coated. Adjust seasonings. Refrigerate for at least 4 hours before serving. **Serves 8.**

BLACK-EYED PEA CORNBREAD

1 (15.5-ounce) can black-eyed peas seasoned with bacon and jalapeno pepper, do not drain
1 cup cornmeal
½ cup flour
1 teaspoon soda
2 eggs, slightly beaten
1 cup buttermilk
½ cup oil
½ pound cheddar cheese, grated
1 onion, chopped
¾ cup cream-style corn
1 pound ground beef, browned and drained
~ picante sauce

Mix all ingredients except picante sauce. Pour into a greased 9 x 13 x 2-inch pan. Bake at 350° for 45 minutes. Let cool about 15 minutes before cutting. Cut into squares to serve. Top each square with picante sauce if desired.

SUMMER IN THE DEEP SOUTH

SUGAR CRUST CAKE

- 1 cup butter
- 2 cups sugar
- 6 eggs
- 2 cups self-rising flour
- 1½ teaspoons vanilla
- 1 teaspoon lemon extract
- ~ powdered sugar

Cream butter and sugar. Add eggs one at a time. Add flour, vanilla, and lemon extract. Pour into a greased and floured bundt pan. Bake at 350° for 1 hour. Cool. Remove from pan and sprinkle with powdered sugar.

PEACH ICE CREAM

- 1 quart peaches, peeled
- 2½ cups sugar
- ~ juice of 1 lemon
- 1 quart whole milk
- ⅔ cup buttermilk
- 1 pint whipping cream

Mash peaches. Add sugar and lemon juice. Let stand 30 minutes. Add milk, buttermilk, and whipping cream. Pour into container of ice cream freezer. Freeze according to manufacturer's instructions.

Today Vicksburgers associate Mississippi mud with a fabulous dessert, but just imagine how strange it was years ago to name a dessert after that thick, oozy river bottom. I know how it happened. My family owned the old Hotel Vicksburg and we had a wonderful chef named Percy Tolliver. One of his specialties was a frozen chocolate pie. Well, you can probably figure out where this is going. A little waitress, Jenny Meyer, who had moved here from Greenville after the 1927 flood, was serving Percy's pie one day. Now to serve Percy's pie you had to be quick – remember it was the 1920s and a restaurant kitchen in Mississippi was probably the hottest place on earth. So, Jenny rushed around trying to cut it, place it on a plate, and run put it in front of the customer before the whole thing melted. Apparently she wasn't very quick that day, because on her way out of the kitchen she quipped that it was beginning to look like Mississippi mud. And there you have it. After we closed the old hotel, we opened Delta Point Restaurant overlooking the River and, of course, served Mississippi Mud Pie. In 1985, the recipe appeared in the Junior Auxiliary's first cookbook, Vintage Vicksburg. We make it just about the same way. This is our recipe.

MISSISSIPPI MUD PIE

- ½ cup butter, melted
- ½ (8 ½-ounce) package chocolate wafers, crushed
- 1 quart vanilla or coffee ice cream
- 1½ cups fudge sauce, chilled
- ~ whipped cream
- ~ chopped pecans and chocolate curls for garnish

Melt butter in large frying pan over low heat; add crushed wafers and toss in butter to coat. Press crumb mixture in a 9-inch pie plate. Cool. Spoon softened ice cream onto crust. Freeze until firm. Top with cold fudge sauce. Store in freezer 8 to 10 hours. Remove from freezer and allow to stand 5 to 10 minutes before serving. To serve, top with whipped cream, pecans, and chocolate curls. **Yield: 6 to 8 servings.**
Mary Frances Dent Terry

The Mississippi River

The Galleries

Visitors entering the circular drive of this 1850 Greek Revival raised cottage are greeted with two coolly bubbling fountains which make them forget the hot Vicksburg sun. Boxwood pathways, lacy crepe myrtles, and over four hundred daylilies blooming yellow, melon, and orange lead to the brick pillars and wooden columns that surround the house and give it its name, The Galleries, home of Jane and Lee Davis Thames.

"When we undertook this continuing project of restoration," Mrs. Thames said, "we knew we wanted a comfortable home where we could rear our seven children – sofas they could sit on, wide plank pine floors they could dance on." And indeed, it is just that. Architect S. J. "Skippy" Tuminello, contractor J. B. Strickland, brick masons, and other local artisans undertook the extensive restoration.

The house boasts fifteen-foot ceilings and five working fireplaces. Almost all the windows contain their original glass. New wide pine flooring was introduced in the downstairs, while the second and third stories kept the original planking.

The thirty-eight-foot-tall entrance foyer with its elegantly curved oval stairway soars to the third story and is accented by a unique double chandelier. One of the most interesting antiques in the home is the focal point of the foyer. It is a cotton sampling table made of Eastern white pine that came from a local cotton company, Melsheimers. Farmers displayed their cotton samples on this table to be graded for selling. The original kitchen was an outbuilding. Moved inside, its cabinets are cypress from the Davis family plantation, Altorf, near Eagle Lake, and old barns in that area. Mrs. Thames says they are wonderful and showed no little fingerprints from their children and now, their grandchildren.

A native of Richmond, Mrs. Thames brought much of her Virginia heritage with her. The home abounds in oriental rugs, period furniture, and family mementoes. An English pine corner cabinet displays a three-generation collection of antique Rose Medallion china. The Tidewater influence permeates The Galleries from its formal gardens to the Smithfield ham and biscuits that appear at all Thames functions. What an elegant setting for any celebration, particularly a Southern tea.

Mrs. Thames says, "There are many special things about our home. Now when our children come home and bring their children, they know it will be just as it was when they were growing up here at The Galleries."

Martha Hickman Day

A SOUTHERN TEA

The one absolute must at a Vicksburg tea is a little round sandwich that has gained national recognition with its own chapter, "The Vicksburg Tomato Sandwich," in A Southern Belle Primer by Maryln Schwartz.

Georgia Street Squares
Sweetheart Cookies
Orange Cream Cake
Sugared Pecans
Garden Vegetable Spread on Zucchini
Date-Nut Chicken Salad Sandwiches
Tee's Cheese Straws
Vicksburg Tomato Sandwiches
Basil Biscuits with Smithfield Ham
Raspberry Citrus Punch

GEORGIA STREET SQUARES

1 cup plus 2 tablespoons butter, divided
1/4 cup sugar
3 teaspoons cocoa
1 slightly beaten egg
3 cups crushed graham crackers
1 cup flaked coconut or 1 cup chopped pecans
2 cups powdered sugar
2 heaping tablespoons vanilla instant pudding and pie filling
1/4 cup milk
2 (1-ounce) squares unsweetened chocolate

Heat 1/2 cup butter, sugar, cocoa, and egg over low heat until butter melts. Cool slightly. Place graham cracker crumbs and coconut or pecans in the bowl of food processor. Process while pouring butter mixture through top of processor. Process until thoroughly combined. Pat firmly in a 9 x 13 x 2-inch pan. Cream 1/2 cup butter, powdered sugar, and pudding. Add milk. Beat until smooth. Spread over graham cracker layer. Refrigerate while preparing the third layer. Melt chocolate and 2 tablespoons butter. Spread over pudding layer. Refrigerate dessert until ready to serve. Cut into squares. Store leftovers in refrigerator. Freezes beautifully. Let thaw in refrigerator before cutting into squares.

TOP: Family silver service on sideboard.
LEFT: Georgia Street Squares and marzipan.
RIGHT: Antique Rose Medallion in pine and cherry cabinet from the 1800s in dining room.

SWEETHEART COOKIES

1½ cups flour
1 cup powdered sugar
¼ teaspoon baking powder
¼ teaspoon salt
5½ ounces coarsely chopped almonds
1 stick unsalted butter, softened
1 egg
1 tablespoon plus 2 teaspoons milk
1 teaspoon vanilla extract
½ teaspoon almond extract
~ raspberry jam
~ powdered sugar

Mix together flour, sugar, baking powder, and salt. Add almonds. In separate bowl beat the butter until fluffy. Add egg, milk, and extracts to the butter mixture. Combine flower and butter mixtures. Gather into a ball, wrap in plastic wrap, and chill for several hours. Preheat oven to 350°. Divide dough in half. On a floured surface roll out dough to a 1/8-inch thickness. Cut out dough with a 2 3/4-inch, heart-shaped cookie cutter. Cut a 1 1/4-inch heart out of the center of half the cookies. Bake for 12 to 15 minutes on an ungreased cookie sheet. Cool on a wire rack. Spread jam on the cookies without the cut-out center. Then place a cut-out cookie on top. Sift powdered sugar on top of each cookie. Makes 24 cookies.

ORANGE CREAM CAKE

1 box yellow cake mix
4 eggs
¼ cup oil
¼ cup applesauce
1 (11-ounce) can mandarin oranges (do not drain)
1 (8-ounce) container of non-dairy whipped topping
1 (3-ounce) box vanilla instant pudding and pie filling
1 (15-ounce) can crushed pineapple, drained

Preheat oven to 325°. Grease and flour two 9-inch cake pans. Combine cake mix, eggs, oil, applesauce, and mandarin oranges with juice. Mix for 2 minutes with electric mixer at medium speed. Pour batter into prepared pans and bake for 25 to 30 minutes. Let cool completely before frosting. Combine whipped topping and pudding mix; stir until well blended. Fold in pineapple. Frost between layers and top and sides of cake. Store cake in refrigerator.

SUGARED PECANS

3 egg whites
¼ cup water
2 cups sugar
½ teaspoon salt
2 tablespoons cinnamon
2 teaspoons powdered allspice
1 teaspoon powdered ginger
1 teaspoon powdered nutmeg
1 ¼ pounds pecan halves

Whisk together egg whites and water. Add sugar, salt, cinnamon, allspice, ginger, and nutmeg. Whisk to blend well. Add the pecans to the egg white mixture, stirring to coat all of the pecans. Spread on a cookie sheet with edges. Bake at 325° until the pecans are crispy, about 20 minutes, stirring after 10 minutes. Spread onto waxed paper which has been placed over layers of newspaper. Let cool. Store in an airtight container. **Yield: 2 pounds candy.**

GARDEN VEGETABLE SPREAD

2 cucumbers, peeled and finely chopped
2 carrots, peeled and finely chopped
1 cup celery, finely chopped
1 small onion, finely chopped
½ green bell pepper, finely chopped
2 (8-ounce) packages cream cheese
1 teaspoon lemon juice
1½ teaspoons salt, divided
¼ to ½ teaspoon red pepper
~ stuffed green olives, sliced
~ zucchini slices

Combine the chopped vegetables in a large colander. Sprinkle with 1 teaspoon of salt. Set colander in a large bowl. Cover and refrigerate overnight so the vegetables can drain. Beat cream cheese until smooth. Mix in lemon juice, salt, red pepper, and vegetables. Chill. Serve spread on zucchini slices or use as a sandwich spread. Garnish with stuffed green olive slices. Keeps several days in the refrigerator. **Yield: 5 to 6 cups.**

TOP: **A plate with a little of everything from the table.**
BOTTOM: **Fifth-generation Davis family garden bench.**
OPPOSITE, RIGHT: **Dining room set for a tea.**

DATE-NUT CHICKEN SALAD SANDWICHES

1   cup chicken, cooked and
    diced
¼   cup dates, finely chopped
¼   cup pecans, chopped
1   cup bacon, crumbled
½   cup mayonnaise
¼   teaspoon salt
~   brown bread or celery
    pieces

Mix chicken, dates, pecans, 1/2 cup
bacon, mayonnaise, and salt. Spread on
brown bread, trim crusts, and cut into
desired shapes, or spoon into celery
pieces. Sprinkle remaining 1/2 cup
bacon on top. **Yield: 3 cups.**

TEE'S CHEESE STRAWS

1   pound extra sharp cheese
2   sticks margarine
3   cups all-purpose flour
1   teaspoon salt
3   tablespoons cold water
½   teaspoon red pepper
~   paprika

Let cheese and margarine stand at room
temperature for several hours until very
soft. Mix cheese and margarine in food
processor. Add remaining ingredients.
Using an electric or manual cookie press
fitted with a standard decorating tip,
press the dough onto an ungreased
cookie sheet. Press the dough through
in a continuous motion, pulling on the
dough so that the straws come out as
thin as possible. Bake at 375° for 12
minutes or until the ends are just
turning brown. Sprinkle with paprika.
Let cool and store in an airtight
container.

The Galleries

ABOVE: Cotton sampling table in the foyer.
RIGHT: Confederate seal and family miniatures on a mahogany secretary.
OPPOSITE, ABOVE: Daylilies.

VICKSBURG TOMATO SANDWICHES

4 loaves day-old bread
6 to 8 medium tomatoes, peeled
~ salt to taste
~ black pepper to taste
~ Homemade Mayonnaise
1 grated onion with juice
~ paprika

Cut bread with biscuit cutter into 72 rounds. Slice tomatoes thinly and place on double sheets of paper towels to drain. Salt and pepper tomato slices. Spread mayonnaise on bread rounds. Place well-drained tomato slices on half the bread rounds and sprinkle again with salt and pepper. Sprinkle 1/2 teaspoon onion with juice over each tomato and top with remaining bread rounds. Sprinkle with paprika. To store until serving time, place on cookie sheet; put waxed paper between layers. Cover tightly and store in refrigerator. **Yield: 36 sandwiches.**

HOMEMADE MAYONNAISE:

1½ tablespoons vegetable oil
1 to 1½ heaping teaspoons Dijon mustard
1 teaspoon salt
1 whole egg plus 1 egg yolk
4 shakes Tabasco
1½ cups vegetable oil
~ juice of one lemon or ¼ cup lemon concentrate

Combine first 5 ingredients in food processor blender. Blend 45 seconds to 1 minute. Gradually add oil with processor running until mixture thickens. When thick, turn off and add lemon juice. Mix well. **Yield: 2 cups.**

BASIL BISCUITS

1 cup all-purpose flour
1½ teaspoons baking powder
¼ teaspoon salt
3 tablespoons cold unsalted butter, cut into pieces
2 tablespoons chopped fresh basil
1½ teaspoons minced shallots
⅓ cup milk

Preheat the oven to 450°. In a large bowl sift together the flour, baking powder, and salt. Cut in the butter until the mixture resembles coarse meal. Stir in the basil and shallots; mix well. Make a well in the center of the flour mixture and pour in the milk. Using a fork, quickly stir to combine. Turn the dough out onto a lightly floured surface. Quickly roll out the dough 1/2-inch thick. Using a lightly-floured, 1-inch round cutter, cut out biscuits. Arrange on an ungreased baking sheet and bake for 12 to 15 minutes or until golden on top and dry on the sides. **Makes approximately 15 biscuits.**

SUMMER IN THE DEEP SOUTH

RASPBERRY CITRUS PUNCH

1 cup raspberries
2 cups sugar
4 cups water
8 cups orange juice, strained
2 (46-ounce) cans pineapple juice
1 (46-ounce) can grapefruit juice
2 quarts soda water, chilled
2 quarts ginger ale, chilled

Force raspberries through a sieve to remove seeds. Combine sugar and water in saucepan. Bring to a boil and boil until sugar is dissolved to make a simple syrup. Combine orange juice, raspberries, pineapple juice, grapefruit juice, and simple syrup. Chill. When ready to serve, add soda water and ginger ale. Serves 100.

An innocent young bride, Libby Horn, moved to Vicksburg from Clinton. Naturally she wanted to do everything correctly, so she joined a garden club. Of course, that was when the garden clubs had high tea; they didn't garden, they just attended, and partied, and laid all the silver out. Libby's first task was to make three dozen tomato sandwiches for an afternoon soirée. In her native town, a tomato sandwich was merely a homely tomato sandwich without pedigree. She took to the party three dozen thick, square sandwiches, WITH THE CRUST ON, peels intact, slathered in store-bought mayonnaise. She said to me, "I was ostracized for two and a half years."

Mary Ruth Smith Jones

George Abraham started making tomato sandwiches for the annual Christmas party he and his wife, Mable, hosted for about 40 years. He didn't know he was taking on a lifelong commitment. Today he is badgered with constant requests for his tomato sandwiches. The shocking part is that his recipe flies in the face of tradition. He doesn't use homemade mayonnaise. Here's how he constructs his famous tomato sandwiches:

"Pick good, large tomatoes. The secret is to give enough tomato. Drop them in boiling water for 28 seconds – not 27, not 29, exactly 28 seconds. Peel the skin off and then slice. Mix one quart of bought mayonnaise (but for goodness sake do buy a good brand!) with one grated onion and three squeezes of lemon juice. Cut white bread in rounds. A Folger's coffee can makes a good cutter. You're really good if they are big round slices with no crust on the edges. Spread the mayonnaise mixture on both slices of bread. Don't be skimpy; this is for your friends, you know. Be sure to sprinkle paprika lightly over the tops."

Harley Halpin Caldwell

The Galleries

Flowerree

Walking the steep stairway of Flowerree Mansion in the early 1960s, a young Vicksburg architect was in the process of fulfilling a boyhood dream.

S. J. "Skip" Tuminello had grown up just around the corner from the mansion built on a bluff overlooking the Mississippi River. In 1961, Tuminello and his wife Gayle, both students in New Orleans, purchased Flowerree.

In those days the area was a happy reflection of European flavors – French, German, Italian, and English families.

"It was an area rich in heritage, inhabited by the city's working people," said Tuminello, today a highly-respected Southern architect.

The couple married in 1955 and lived in Tuminello's boyhood home, Annabelle, while working on Flowerree.

"I knew we could never afford to build a home such as this one – of a different era with so many features I wanted. As a designer, I was just too critical. Here was the best that could be done."

The house, built by Colonel Charles Conway Flowerree, was completed in 1872 and boasted 10,000 square feet. He was the army's youngest full colonel at age nineteen. A Virginian, he married a Vicksburg woman, Jennie Wilson, and made Vicksburg his home, where he and his wife raised six children; the last of their heirs remained in the city until 1929.

The Tuminellos and their two sons and daughter have dedicated years to the restoration of the grand, high-ceiling Victorian Italianate home.

For Skippy Tuminello, the dreams of creating and renovating buildings came early. When he was a young boy in his hometown by the river, Tuminello built masterful replicas of local sites – St. Paul Catholic Church, Cedar Grove, and the Old Court House. The bricks for his boyhood creations were made of mud and baked in his mother's oven. For colored glass, the architect-in-the-making used bits of blue from broken magnesia bottles. Wooden spools that once held his grandmother's threads became columns.

Since he and his wife became the owners of Flowerree, projects from replacing an initial leaking roof to the complete renovation of the kitchen have taken up the time and talents of the Tuminellos.

The house was in a state of disrepair and deterioration when first the Tuminellos took charge.

"We just got busy and started scrubbing," Gayle Tuminello said.

And in the midst of the toil, treasures were discovered.

"There were old uniforms of Colonel Flowerree, small toys, pottery, and some porcelain." Tiny treasures in the closets of an enormous treasure.

Martha Hickman Day

AN ITALIAN DINNER

"Hey, Domonique, what did Mary fix for you today?" Those were the words railroad men called out daily as the grocery store owner lunched outside in 1899. A lucky few were invited to join him; and eventually the grocery business gave way to the opening of the restaurant that would become famous, Tuminello's. Skip and Gayle Tuminello have carried on his grandparents' tradition of serving classic Italian fare on Vicksburg's finest tables.

Bellini Cocktails
Artichoke Cheesecake
Orange and Black Olive Salad
Baked Salmon
Grilled Vegetables
Espresso Granita

ABOVE: Orange and Black Olive Salad is served.
RIGHT: Dining room table set for dinner with 1840-era soft paste china. Chandelier designed by Mr. Tuminello.

BELLINI COCKTAILS

2 ounces peach nectar
1 teaspoon fresh lemon juice
1 ounce peach schnapps
~ crushed ice
3 ounces chilled dry champagne

Mix the peach nectar, lemon juice, and schnapps in a chilled glass. Add 1/2 cup (or more) crushed ice and stir. Add champagne. Yield: 2 servings. (May be prepared in a blender to produce a frozen drink.)

ARTICHOKE CHEESECAKE

2 tablespoons butter, softened
¼ cup fine dry breadcrumbs
¼ cup Parmesan cheese (grated)
2 tablespoons Italian seasoning
2 (8-ounce) packages cream cheese at room temperature
1 cup crumbled feta cheese
3 large eggs
1 cup sour cream
1 (14-ounce) can artichoke hearts, drained and chopped
1 small red bell pepper, chopped
1 small green bell pepper, chopped
6 scallion heads, plus ½-inch green tops from each, chopped
1 large clove garlic, pressed
1 teaspoon crushed dried tarragon
1 tablespoon fresh or dried basil

Grease a 9-inch springform pan with the butter. Mix together the breadcrumbs, Parmesan cheese, and 2 tablespoons Italian seasoning. Coat bottom of pan; set aside remaining mixture. Preheat oven to 375°. In food processor beat cream cheese until fluffy. Add feta cheese, eggs, and sour cream. Beat until smooth. Add chopped artichokes. Beat in red and green bell peppers, scallions, garlic, tarragon, and basil. Spoon mixture into prepared pan. Bake for 40 minutes or until golden brown. Cool to room temperature. Chill for at least 2 hours. Remove from pan. Pat reserved crumb coating mixture on outside of cheesecake. Serve with toast points or crackers. Yield: one cheesecake.

TOP: Collection of bronze and brass statues.
RIGHT: Parlour with pierced plasterwork molding.

ORANGE AND BLACK OLIVE SALAD

- ~ curly leaf lettuce
- 4 salad oranges, peeled and sectioned, or 1 jar salad oranges, drained
- 1 can black pitted olives
- 1/2 cup olive oil
- 1/2 cup balsamic vinegar
- ~ fresh lime juice
- ~ salt and pepper
- 1 red onion, sliced thinly and separated into rings

Chill all ingredients before assembling individual salads. For each serving, place lettuce on plate. Divide orange wedges and black olives among salad plates. Combine olive oil and vinegar. Drizzle over salads. Squeeze lime juice over each salad and sprinkle with salt and pepper. Top with onion slices.
Yield: 8 servings.

GRILLED VEGETABLES

- 4 yellow squash
- 4 zucchini squash
- 6 large carrots, scraped
- 1 large red onion
- 1/4 cup olive oil
- 2 tablespoons tarragon vinegar
- 1 clove garlic, crushed
- 1/4 teaspoon dried thyme
- 1/4 teaspoon salt
- 1/4 teaspoon pepper
- ~ chopped fresh basil

Slice squash, zucchini, and carrots into lengthwise strips about 1/4-inch thick. Slice onion into 1/4-inch slices. Place vegetables into large bowl and toss with remaining ingredients. Cook vegetables on a hot grill and sear lightly; turn vegetables over. Cook until vegetables get limp, but are still al dente, about 8 to 10 minutes. Place on a serving platter and sprinkle with chopped fresh basil. Serves 8.

BAKED SALMON

- 1 large salmon fillet
- 1/2 cup extra virgin olive oil
- 1/4 cup lemon juice
- 1 tablespoon wine vinegar
- 1/3 cup minced onion
- 1 teaspoon dried tarragon leaves
- 1/4 teaspoon black pepper

Place salmon in a large, shallow glass pan. In a small bowl combine olive oil, lemon juice, vinegar, onion, tarragon, and black pepper with a wire whisk. Pour over salmon. Marinate at room temperature for 30 minutes. Turn salmon and marinate 30 minutes more. Bake salmon at 375° for 30 minutes or until fish flakes when tested with a fork.

TOP: **Artichoke Cheesecake.**
BOTTOM, FAR LEFT: **Walnut and English burled walnut newel post with tile inlays.**
BOTTOM, LEFT: **Brass and gold leaf hinge.**

Flowerree

TOP, LEFT: Bronze Regency candelabra and collection of breakfast cups on sideboard. Tea service is of old New Orleans coin silver.
ABOVE: Capital from home of Newit Vick, founder of Vicksburg.
LEFT: The garden.
BELOW: Period Regency bronze oil lamp.
OPPOSITE PAGE: Bellini Cocktails on the old-brick terrace.

ESPRESSO GRANITA

- 1/2   cup sugar
- 2   tablespoons water
- 6   cups espresso
- 2   teaspoons unsweetened cocoa powder
- 1   pint whipping cream, whipped with 3 tablespoons powdered sugar
- ~   nutmeg
- ~   mint leaves

Combine the sugar and water in a saucepan and stir until sugar is dissolved. Boil the syrup for several minutes. Pour the espresso into the syrup, dissolve the cocoa into the syrup mixture, and remove from heat. Let cool completely. Pour this mixture into a bowl and freeze until solid. Transfer to a blender and process for a few seconds until slushy. Spoon into parfait glasses — a layer of granita, then a layer of whipped cream. Repeat layers. Sprinkle with nutmeg and garnish with mint sprigs. Serves 8.

SUMMER IN THE DEEP SOUTH

When my sister Khaki was going into the convent, a friend of the family decided to give her a party – you know, like a debutante – same thing, okay? When we got to the party, everything was beautiful. Drop-dead, gorgeous silver and just so much of it – a beautiful table, until you really looked. Then you realized that the food was quite curious. Peanuts, potato chips, things off the grocery store shelf. And the pièce de résistance – an incredible silver chafing dish filled with canned ravioli. We were astonished and, as it turns out, lucky. This same lady once gave a party with all her silver laid out but forgot the food. Best of all, she never noticed.

Harley Halpin Caldwell

I lived in California most of my life but always spent several weeks of the summer in Vicksburg at my aunt and uncle's home. Over the years, I made lots of friends and had a grand time going to bridge and parties and catching up on everyone. But the one thing I never did get use to was the "Coke Parties." This was in the 1950s; and all the ladies would dress up in their hats and summer dresses and high heels and white gloves and go to parties and drink Coca-Colas – straight out of the bottle. I guess it was a logical, Southern answer to high tea; but it sure did look silly.

Leone Templeton Dingman

To old-time Vicksburgers, the Fourth of July is not a day to be celebrated. Since Vicksburg surrendered to General Ulysses S. Grant on July 4, 1863, after 47 days of siege, that holiday was not celebrated in Vicksburg until 1945 at the end of Work War II. Even after that, it was not celebrated with any regularity or to any extent until recent years. And the celebrations we do have are still low-key – a few small gatherings or cookouts at nearby lake homes or in neighborhoods. In fact, many old-time Vicksburgers simply don't think of The Fourth as a time to celebrate. So don't come here looking for a parade. We'll show you a great re-enactment. And, of course, in our version the Rebels always win!

Dannie Compton Weatherly

Flowerree

Harris Dickson House

It has been said, "When Judge Harris Dickson lived in his home at the top of Mulvihill Street, it was about the liveliest place in town." Dickson was a nationally – and internationally – known writer and storyteller. He was born in 1868 in Yazoo City, but grew up in Meridian and Vicksburg.

What an interesting fellow he was. His friends ranged from Buffalo Bill to Edward VIII, then the Prince of Wales. His travels stretched across Europe and to places as far away as Africa. And he served one short term as municipal court judge, forever labeling him as Judge Dickson.

As a writer of novels and short stories, Dickson ignored popular trends and continued to write in the romantic style. And although he lived on Mulvihill, he traveled easily and often to his writers' clubs in New York City. One of his favorites was the Players' Club. He was a war correspondent for *Collier's Magazine*, but was best known as a serial writer for *The Saturday Evening Post*.

The *Black Wolf's Breed* was the first of his fourteen novels and his most popular novel nationally was *Old Reliable*. But the book most popular in this region was *Old-Fashioned Senator*, a friendly portrait of John Sharp Williams after his retirement. The story is told that when Dickson sat down to interview the reluctant senator for the book, the senator told him to put away his pad and pencil. The only thing he wanted on the table was whiskey. The result was, thankfully, all remembered and recorded by Dickson.

The two-story stucco, Prairie-style house built in 1908 was built specifically for Dickson. The downstairs was designed to entertain – something the Dicksons did often and well. But with all of Dickson's entertaining personality pouring from the house, there is one room that quite possibly was his soul – the writer's library. Dark paneling, a tremendous brick fireplace, tall, glassed-in bookcases – it is so easy to imagine his working there. And to imagine the night when, after struggling with a manuscript, he said to his wife Madeleine, "Darling, the words just won't come anymore." He then threw his last manuscript into the roaring fire.

The house was sold in 1946 to the Hardy family, and then in 1958 to the D. P. Waring family. Today, it is owned by the Robert Bailess family. Mrs. Bailess, the former Natalie Waring, grew up in the Harris Dickson house. The Bailesses have undertaken a great deal of restoration, but the stately character of the home still reigns.

It is a warm, friendly house at the top of Mulvihill that has carried on the Dickson tradition and now the Bailess tradition of family, laughter, and gathering of good friends.

Martha Hickman Day

THE MISS MISSISSIPPI PAGEANT PARTY

Vicksburg has been proud to host the Miss Mississippi Scholarship Pageant since 1958. A summer week that has been referred to as Vicksburg's "Mardi Gras" is enjoyed by the town while the entire state looks on. A Broadway-style production, autograph parties, pre-pageant parties, and four nights in a row of after-pageant parties have all helped this small town to send four Miss Mississippis on to become Miss Americas.

Beef Tenderloin with Horseradish Mayonnaise
Southern Yeast Rolls
Crawfish Strudel
Glazed Cheese
Checkerboard Cheese
Kahlua Mousse in Miniature Mergingue Shells
Cheesecake Squares
Lemon Dip for Fresh Fruit

BEEF TENDERLOIN WITH HORSERADISH MAYONNAISE

1	(5 to 6 pound) beef tenderloin
2	cups port wine
1/2	cup olive oil
1	small onion, chopped
2	cloves garlic, minced
3	bay leaves
~	salt and pepper
~	Horseradish Mayonnaise

Combine port wine, olive oil, onion, garlic, bay leaves, salt, and pepper. Pour over beef and marinate overnight. Preheat oven to 425°. Remove beef from marinade and pat dry. Bake on a rack in a shallow roasting pan for 45 to 50 minutes or until meat thermometer reaches 150° for medium rare. Slice thinly and serve with Horseradish Mayonnaise.

HORSERADISH MAYONNAISE:

1	cup heavy cream
1	cup mayonnaise
~	pinch of salt
1/4	cup horseradish

Whip cream. Combine with mayonnaise and salt until well blended. Add horseradish, mixing well. **Yield: 2 cups.**

TOP: **Original drawing from a Saturday Evening Post story by Dickson and copies of his books.**
ABOVE: clockwise from left: Crawfish Strudel, Kahlua Mousse in Miniature Meringue Shells, fresh fruit and Lemon Dip, Glazed Cheeses, and Checkerboard Cheese on an 1815 American Sheraton sideboard.

SOUTHERN YEAST ROLLS

4 cups flour
1 teaspoon salt
1/2 cup sugar
1 cup Crisco
3 eggs, beaten slightly
1 (1/4-ounce) package of yeast dissolved in 1/4 cup lukewarm water (105 to 115°)
1 cup lukewarm milk (105 to 115°)
~ melted butter

Sift together flour, salt, and sugar. Cut in Crisco until dry mixture resembles coarse grain. Mix eggs, yeast, milk, and flour mixture. DO NOT KNEAD. Cover and refrigerate overnight. Take out 2 hours before using and let rise in a warm, draft-free place. Work dough into smooth ball and roll out to 1/4-inch thickness on well-floured surface. Cut into small circles. With the back of a knife, crease circles slightly to one side of center. Dip circles in melted butter and fold larger half of circle over small. Place on buttered baking sheet and let rise until doubled in size, about 1 to 2 hours. Bake in 400° oven for 12 to 15 minutes.

CRAWFISH STRUDEL

2 1/2 pounds crawfish tails
4 shallots, chopped
1 large onion, chopped
1/2 cup butter
2 cloves garlic, minced
1/2 cup white wine
1/2 cup whipping cream
~ salt and pepper to taste
8 dozen purchased phyllo pastry shells
1 small Brie cheese
8 ounces finely shredded Monterey Jack cheese

Cook crawfish, shallots, and onion in butter, garlic, and white wine for approximately 3 minutes. Add whipping cream and cook until liquid reduces, approximately 30 minutes. Add salt and pepper. Place pastry shells on a cookie sheet. Place a small piece of Brie in the bottom of each pastry shell. Fill each shell with crawfish mixture and top with Monterey Jack. Bake at 375° for 8 to 10 minutes. **Yield: 8 dozen appetizers.** (This recipe halves easily for smaller parties).

GLAZED CHEESE

2 cups dry white wine
1 envelope unflavored gelatin flat-surfaced cheeses (any rinds must be edible)
~ pesticide-free edible flowers and herbs

Combine wine and gelatin in a saucepan and let stand for 5 minutes. Place over medium heat and stir until gelatin is completely dissolved and mixture is clear. Place pan in a large container of ice water. Stir gently, occasionally, until it begins to thicken and look syrupy. If mixture becomes too firm, reheat and chill again until syrupy. Place cold cheese on a wire rack in a shallow pan. Arrange flowers and herbs on the surface of your cheese to determine your desired pattern. Remove and set aside. Using a feather pastry brush spread a coat of the gelatin over the top and sides of the cheese. When slightly tacky to touch, about 1 to 4 minutes, replace flowers and herbs. Refrigerate for 20 minutes. Apply a second coat of gelatin and return cheese to the refrigerator for 20 minutes. Apply 1 or 2 more coats of gelatin to

completely cover decorations. Refrigerate after each coat. Refrigerate until ready to serve, up to 36 hours. Unused glaze may be refrigerated, covered, for several weeks. Recipe yields enough glaze to coat 6 (3 x 5-inch) rectangles of cheese with 3 layers of glaze.

TOP, LEFT: **Sugared fruit.** TOP: **Fruit, Glazed Cheeses, and Checkerboard Cheese.** LEFT: **Mantel in the dining room.** ABOVE: **In the library.**
OPPOSITE PAGE: **Glorious flowers.**

CHECKERBOARD CHEESE

1/2 cup olive oil
1/2 cup white wine vinegar
1 (2-ounce) jar diced pimiento, drained
3 tablespoons chopped parsley
4 tablespoons chopped green onion
3 cloves garlic, pressed
1 teaspoon sugar
1 teaspoon dried basil
1/2 teaspoon salt
1/2 teaspoon pepper
1 (8-ounce) block sharp cheddar cheese, chilled
1 (8-ounce) package cream cheese, chilled

Combine all ingredients except the cheeses. Cut each block of cheese into thirds, lengthwise. Cut each strip into small squares. Alternate the squares of cheese to form a checkerboard pattern on a serving platter with sides to contain the marinade. Pour marinade over cheese and refrigerate at least 6 to 8 hours before serving. Serve with assorted crackers.

KAHLUA MOUSSE

1 pound dark sweet chocolate
3 ounces butter
1/2 cup sifted powdered sugar
3 egg yolks
1/4 cup Kahlua
2 cups whipping cream
3 egg whites

Melt chocolate and butter together. In large bowl combine powdered sugar, egg yolks, and Kahlua. Blend chocolate mixture into this. In another bowl whip cream until stiff and gently fold into chocolate mixture. Blend well. Beat egg whites until soft peaks form and fold into chocolate cream. Refrigerate overnight. Serve in goblets or in bite-size meringues for a pick-up dessert.

MINIATURE MERINGUE SHELLS

8 egg whites
1/4 teaspoon cream of tartar
1/8 teaspoon salt
2 cups sugar

Preheat oven to 225°. Beat egg whites until frothy. Add the cream of tartar and salt and beat until mixture holds soft peaks. Continue beating, gradually adding sugar, until the whites hold stiff peaks. Line a baking sheet with parchment paper. Form shells by spooning a dollop of the mixture onto the cookie sheet and with the back of a teaspoon shaping into shells about an inch in diameter with an indentation in the center. Bake for 1 hour; then turn oven off and leave in oven for another 30 minutes. Note: Meringues must be made on a sunny day or they will weep.

CHEESECAKE SQUARES

1/2 cup margarine
1/3 cup brown sugar
3/4 cup pecans, chopped
1 cup all-purpose flour
3 (8-ounce) packages cream cheese
1 1/2 cups sugar
3 eggs
1 1/2 tablespoons lemon juice
1 1/2 tablespoons vanilla extract
~ Sour Cream Topping
~ fresh fruit

In bowl of food processor process margarine, brown sugar, pecans, and flour. Press into a greased 9 x 13 x 2-inch pan. Bake 10 minutes at 350°. Beat cream cheese with sugar. Add eggs, lemon juice, and vanilla. Pour over crust. Bake at 350° for 30 minutes. Cool and refrigerate. Cut into small squares to serve. Top each square with a dollop of Sour Cream Topping and a small piece of fresh fruit. Blueberries, kiwi, mandarin oranges, and strawberries work well.

SOUR CREAM TOPPING:

1 cup sour cream
1 teaspoon vanilla extract
1 1/2 tablespoons sugar

Combine all ingredients in a small bowl.

LEMON DIP FOR FRESH FRUIT

1 (8-ounces) package cream cheese
8 ounces non-dairy whipped topping
1 cup powdered sugar
1 (0.23-ounce) package unsweetened lemonade-flavored drink mix

Beat cream cheese until soft. Beat in whipped topping, powdered sugar, and drink mix. Serve with seasonal fruits.

Harris Dickson House

FALL IN THE DEEP SOUTH

Fall is sweet potato time. And pork chop time. And turnip green time. And it's the time the Mississippi River turns blue. Oh, it's not blue really. It's just as muddy as ever. But the oppressive sun which has made the cotton bolls ripen and burst open and the soybeans dry enough to combine (that's com-bine) and has kept all rational people on their porches under their fans or in their homes under their fans or fanning themselves even as they browse the aisles in their favorite air-conditioned supermarket grocery stores is not arching quite so high across the noontime sky. It's lower. It's less intense. It's gentler and it lets the heavenly blue of heaven itself emerge. And the big old Mississippi, ambling by just as it does during all seasons of the year, can't help but pick up some of that blue and toss it right back. Fall is celebration time down South. Celebration for the harvest, sure. But for more. It's football season and Friday-night friends gather on those tired old bleachers down at the high school to watch their sons scramble and their daughters cheer, kind of, but just as much to talk about who's bringing what to the tailgate gatherings on all the college campuses Saturday morning. Men talk about their deer camps; and men who watch that river, not for color as much as "whether there's enough water for the ducks," look forward to walking in the forests and paddling up the sloughs when it gets, well, just a little bit cooler. Fall. Kids in their colorful coats stand, never still, by the roadsides waiting for the school bus and staring at their breath, which, sometimes, they can see. The pecans are falling. Fill a pocket, take them home, and give them to Mama. "Make me a pie, Mama. Make me a pie." Wash those greens well. If you think you've washed them enough, wash them some more. Don't want any grit. Flavor too strong? Boil them once, pour off that water, add fresh water, and boil them some more. Oh, and add a spoon or so of sugar.

Charlie Mitchell

Charlie Mitchell grew up in Vicksburg, but left to get a bachelor's degree in journalism from Mississippi State University and a law degree from the University of Mississippi. He has been an observer of the city since 1954 and has been writing about it since 1975 for The Vicksburg Post, *where he is now managing editor.*

Cedar Grove Mansion

With its four columns rising two full stories and holding deep galleries that run the width of the house, Cedar Grove, to the passerby, looks exactly like what an antebellum mansion of the Old South should.

But to drive past and gasp at its sheer beauty – and a gasp is the reaction its overpowering presence seems to demand – is to miss something really important. Cedar Grove isn't a museum or some edifice raised by a government to showcase its authority. It is a home. It is an imposing structure, but it has a soft side.

A romantic aspect, and one probably told to all the newlyweds who visit the bed and breakfast each year, is that the home itself was a wedding gift from John Klein to his bride, Elizabeth Day, when it was finished in 1852. And, in keeping with custom among the wealthy of that era, it was furnished, and is still in large measure furnished, with adornment they selected on their bridal trip to Paris.

Now homes have to have practical aspects. It's hard to imagine a structure as imposing as Cedar Grove's being practical. But those deep porches and wide galleries are precisely that. In the decades before air conditioning, they kept the direct sunlight off the exterior walls, allowing them to remain several degrees cooler through the day and through the night.

A piece of furniture inside Cedar Grove proved pretty practical, too. It's a sideboard – or at least it looks like a sideboard – and therein lies its wonderful secret. That secret has been kept for generations by cherubs inset into the piece; and most importantly, the secret was kept during the War Between the States.

The sideboard, you see, is really a safe and is believed to have hidden the treasures and inventory of Klein, a jeweler among other interests, during and after the battle for Vicksburg.

Of course, we now know that it took several attempts and then a siege before Union forces entered the southern stronghold. But day to day for more than two years, the Kleins and other families in the city didn't know if or when those Yankees would arrive. And word had preceded the Union troops: Any property of a known Rebel was subject to seizure. Any property of Unionists who happened to be living in Vicksburg – and there were many – was just as likely to be taken should marauding soldiers start pillaging.

But the cherubs did their duty. The Klein fortune, at least that part hidden in the sideboard, was as safe after the War Between the States as it was before.

Charlie Mitchell

PILGRIMAGE TOUR GUIDES' BRUNCH

Twice a year Vicksburg homeowners are up to their hoop skirts in housekeeping. They fluff up pillows, wax steps, lemon oil furniture, call on their very best friends to help, put on their finest 1800s costume, throw open the doors, and say, "Welcome to Vicksburg. Where are y'all from?" When the two weeks of entertaining and educating are over, it's time for the homeowners to thank those friends who helped to put Vicksburg's best foot forward.

Spinach and Strawberry Salad
Creole Chicken
Garlic Cheese Grits
Cream Cheese Biscuits
Blueberry Skillet Jam

ABOVE: **Console table reflecting hem of antebellum dress.**
RIGHT: **Mr. Klein's disguised safe in the dining room.**

SPINACH AND STRAWBERRY SALAD

1/2	cup sugar
1	tablespoon poppy seeds
2	tablespoons sesame seeds
1 1/2	teaspoons minced onion
1/4	teaspoon paprika
1/4	cup cider vinegar
1/4	cup wine vinegar
1/2	cup oil
2	tablespoons butter
3/4	cup sliced almonds
1	pound spinach, torn into bite-size pieces
1	pint strawberries, sliced

For dressing, mix sugar, poppy seeds, sesame seeds, onion, paprika, vinegars, and oil in a bowl. Whisk to combine thoroughly. In a small skillet melt butter and sauté almonds until lightly brown. Remove from skillet and set aside to cool. Combine spinach, strawberries, and almonds in a large serving bowl. When ready to serve, pour dressing over salad and toss lightly. Serves 6 to 8.

CREOLE CHICKEN

½ cup plus 3 tablespoons flour, divided
½ cup plus 3 tablespoons vegetable oil, divided
1 medium onion, chopped
1 medium green bell pepper, chopped
2 cloves garlic, minced
1 (10¾-ounce) can chicken broth
1 (15-ounce) can tomato sauce
2 bay leaves
1 teaspoon garlic powder
1 teaspoon red pepper
1 teaspoon oregano
1 teaspoon black pepper
½ teaspoon basil
½ teaspoon thyme
2 pounds boneless, skinless chicken breasts, cut into bite-size pieces
~ chicken broth or white wine, if necessary

Combine 1/2 cup flour and 1/2 cup oil in deep pan. Cook over medium-low heat, stirring constantly for 20 minutes or until roux is caramel-colored. Add onion, bell pepper, and garlic and sauté until tender, about 4 minutes. Add chicken broth, tomato sauce, and bay leaves. Cover and simmer over low heat about 20 to 30 minutes, stirring occasionally. Add a little chicken broth or white wine to thin if mixture becomes too thick.

Combine remaining 3 tablespoons flour, garlic powder, red pepper, oregano, black pepper, basil, and thyme in a paper bag. Shake to mix ingredients. Dredge chicken pieces in flour mixture. Heat remaining oil in a non-stick skillet over medium heat. Brown chicken on all

sides in several batches. Remove chicken from skillet and drain well. Add chicken to sauce. Cover and simmer over low heat for 10 to 15 minutes or until thoroughly heated and chicken is done. Remove bay leaves and serve over Garlic Cheese Grits. **Serves 10 to 12.**

GARLIC CHEESE GRITS

7 cups water
1 teaspoon salt
2 cups quick-cooking grits
2 (6-ounce) rolls process cheese with garlic

Bring water to a boil in a large pot. Stir in salt and grits. Return to boil and reduce heat. Simmer until grits are done, about 6 minutes, stirring occasionally. Add cheese and stir until cheese melts. Press grits into a greased 9 x 13 x 2-inch pan. Cover and keep in a warm oven until ready to serve. Cut in squares and spoon Creole Chicken over grits.

CREAM CHEESE BISCUITS

1 cup flour
¼ teaspoon salt
1 teaspoon baking powder
1 tablespoon sugar
1 (3-ounce) package cream cheese
1 stick melted butter

Combine flour, salt, baking powder, and sugar. Cut cream cheese into flour mixture. Stir in melted butter. Roll out dough on a floured surface. Cut with a 1 1/2 inch biscuit cutter. Bake at 400° for 12 to 15 minutes. **Yield: 3 dozen.**

OPPOSITE, FAR LEFT: **Oil painting of the Marquise de Pompadour, mistress of Louis XV.**
OPPOSITE, TOP: **Drapery holdback in the style of Queen Victoria's hand.**
OPPOSITE, BOTTOM: **Brunch in the dining room.**
LEFT: **Settee by famed New Orleans cabinetmaker, Prudent Mallard, in the parlour.**

BLUEBERRY SKILLET JAM

1 **pint blueberries, mashed**
2 **tablespoons powdered fruit pectin**
1/2 **teaspoon margarine or butter**
1 **cup sugar**

In a skillet heat blueberries, pectin, and margarine over medium-high heat, stirring constantly until mixture boils. Stir in sugar; bring back to a boil and boil for 1 minute. Remove from heat. Pour jam into 2 half-pint jars with tight-fitting lids. Cover and refrigerate until jam is set and cold. Keep refrigerated and use within 3 weeks. Yield: **2 cups.**

It was Pilgrimage time, and Vicksburg was teeming with tourists. At the Old Court House Museum, one older lady who was with a tour group walked to the front door, looked toward the street, and gasped, "My bus! Where's my bus?" I pointed out that it was parked at the base of the steps directly in front of the building. "That's not my bus," she said. "My bus was full and that one is empty."

Gordon Cotton

We had a lovely little couple, a little on the country side, take our tour one day. They were looking around and under and through and so concerned about everything. They asked questions and were very appreciative. During the course of our tour I think we say at least four times that Martha Vick died in 1850. After this couple finished the tour, they went down to the Vanishing Glory. Later, Dotti from The Vanishing Glory called and said, "Did you just have two little country people up there?" I said, "Sure did. Lovely people." She said, "They sure were. Loved our show. When they said they had been to your house, I asked if they liked it. They said, 'Oh, we loved it. They were so nice to us. Showed us all around. That place was just chock full of antiques. But, you know, we never did get to meet Martha Vick.'"

Bill Longfellow

1500 China Street – or 15 China – was one of the most famous addresses in the Mississippi Valley and beyond. On the outside, it was a rather simple three-story brick structure; on the inside, it was furnished in the finest style with gilded mirrors, crystal chandeliers, walnut furniture – and pretty girls. Over the decades Vicksburg's houses of ill repute were closed down. Around 1960, 15 China was torn down and the contents sold. Years later as an elderly couple toured one of the antebellum homes in town, they saw a one-of-a-kind elaborate antique bed. The gentleman insisted, "I've seen that bed before." His wife disputed him but he was insistent: "I know I've seen it before. I just can't remember where." The tour guide never told the origin of the bed – 15 China.

Gordon Cotton

Cedar Grove Mansion

The Govenor McNutt House

Of all the antebellum structures remaining in Vicksburg, The Governor McNutt House may be the busiest. It's a school, a private Montessori school, and the youngsters have pretty much the run of the place.

Alexander Gallatin McNutt, the first of three Mississippi governors who have resided in Vicksburg, hailed from Virginia. He started a law practice in Jackson before moving to the then-more-prosperous Vicksburg in 1824, the year before it was incorporated and when Mississippi was just seven years old. Alone and in partnerships, he also owned plantations in Warren and Washington Counties.

He was no fan of banks, including the Planters Bank, located a few blocks away; and after a term in the Senate, he was elected governor in 1837. His two, two-year terms were marked with discord over what constituted fair banking practices. His views and the banks' were often not the same.

But there was a hint of scandal in his own life, at least by today's standards. McNutt jointly owned the 4,000-acre Walnut Hills plantation near the city with Joel Cameron. When Cameron was murdered on the place by slaves, it left his lovely wife, Elizabeth Lewis Cameron, a widow. Within a year, she and McNutt married, and he owned it all.

Perhaps there was no tabloid press in those days. Regardless, eighteen months after his inauguration, McNutt sold his L-shaped Vicksburg home – nearly identical to his mother's still-standing cottage in Rockbridge County, Virginia – with its furnishing for $17,000. Fortune, and perhaps those corrupt banks, did in the buyer, Hugh Dunlop, and the home was sold again to satisfy Dunlop's creditors in 1844. They got only $200, but the buyer really got his money's worth. Hamilton Wright of New Orleans and his descendants continued to own the home and occupy or lease it all the way until 1965. It was then transferred to a historic trust and then again twelve years after to Dr. and Mrs. Hall Whitaker. It was the Whitakers, he a dentist and accomplished watercolorist and she a fan of history and antiques, who undertook restoration of The Governor McNutt House and made it their house and home as well. After about a dozen years, they sold it for use as a school.

One has to believe McNutt would be pleased. The Governor McNutt House is a happy place, full of learning. And there are no longer any banks in the neighborhood either.

Charlie Mitchell

BASKET LUNCH ON THE PLAYGROUND

Things that would be considered odd anywhere else are just part of the everyday routine in Vicksburg. For instance, where else is there a Confederate soldier buried on the playground? There's no resting in peace here though. He teaches the children in his own way about the war, life, and death; he catches a few errant soccer balls with his headstone; and he even provides a subtle suggestion for the perfect schoolhouse kitty name – Lieutenant McGill, of course.

Refreshing Apple Lemonade
Roast Beef in Pita Pockets
Technicolor Pasta Salad
Marinated Apples with Amaretto Spread
Island Cookies
Lunchbox Caramel Bars

REFRESHING APPLE LEMONADE

2 cups Basic Syrup
4 cups apple juice
1 cup fresh lemon juice
4 cups water

Combine all ingredients and serve over ice or serve hot with a cinnamon stick for stirring.

BASIC SYRUP:

4 cups sugar
4 cups water

Combine sugar and water in a saucepan. Bring to a boil and boil 10 minutes.

TOP: **Lunch in front of a new building, the Little Red Schoolhouse.**
LEFT: **A comic-book basket lunch.**

83

ROAST BEEF IN PITA POCKETS

2 pounds cooked roast beef, sliced thinly
1 (8-ounce) carton sour cream
1 teaspoon dried dill weed
1/4 cup green onions, chopped
1/4 cup olive oil
1/4 cup dry red wine
1 tablespoon vinegar
1 teaspoon basil
1/2 teaspoon salt
1 pound fresh mushrooms, sliced
2 large tomatoes, coarsely chopped
1/2 cup green onions, sliced
8 pita pockets

Chill roast beef. Combine sour cream, dill, and chopped green onions. Mix well. Cover and refrigerate dressing several hours or overnight. Combine olive oil, red wine, vinegar, basil, and salt. Mix well. Combine mushrooms, tomatoes, and sliced green onions. Pour olive oil mixture over vegetables and toss. Cover and refrigerate several hours or overnight. To assemble sandwiches, spread the inside of the pita pocket with the sour cream dressing. Place several slices of the roast beef into pita. Top with vegetable mixture. Add more sour cream dressing if desired. Using Cajun spiced roast beef from the deli is a delicious variation for this recipe. **Yield:** 8 pocket sandwiches.

TOP: **Technicolor Pasta Salad.**
BOTTOM: **Where learning skills are taught.**

TECHNICOLOR PASTA SALAD

2 (12-ounce) packages rainbow rotini, cooked al dente
1 bunch broccoli flowerets
6 green onions, chopped
2 ribs celery, chopped
1 can black olives, pitted
3/4 cup stuffed green olives
1 can artichokes
1 green bell pepper, coarsely chopped
1 red bell pepper, coarsely chopped
1 yellow bell pepper, coarsely chopped
1 1/2 tablespoons garlic powder
1 1/2 tablespoons parsley
1 1/2 tablespoons seasoned salt
~ salt and pepper to taste
1/4 cup fresh, grated Parmesan cheese
1 cup olive oil
6 tablespoons apple cider vinegar

Combine all ingredients and mix well. Refrigerate for 24 hours. Serves 14 to 16 or more.

MARINATED APPLES

6 Red Delicious apples
6 Granny Smith apples
1 large can pineapple juice

Wash, core, and slice apples. Place in large bowl. Pour pineapple juice over apples and refrigerate overnight. The apples will not brown and will keep several days in the refrigerator.

AMARETTO SPREAD FOR APPLES

1 (8-ounce) package cream cheese
1/4 cup Amaretto
1/4 to 1/2 cup toasted sliced almonds

Beat cream cheese with Amaretto. Mound mixture in center of serving tray. Decorate top with toasted almonds. Place Marinated Apples around spread.

ISLAND COOKIES

1 2/3 cups all-purpose flour
3/4 teaspoon baking powder
1/2 teaspoon baking soda
1/2 teaspoon salt
3/4 cup butter, softened
1/3 cup sugar
3/4 cup brown sugar, packed
1 teaspoon vanilla extract
1 egg
2 cups milk chocolate chips
1 cup flaked coconut, toasted
1 cup chopped walnuts

Preheat oven to 375°. Combine flour, baking powder, baking soda, and salt. Set aside. Beat butter, sugar, brown sugar, and vanilla until creamy. Beat in egg. Blend in flour mixture. Stir in milk chocolate chips, coconut, and walnuts. Drop by tablespoonfuls onto an ungreased baking sheet. Bake for 8 to 11 minutes or until golden brown. **Makes approximately 5 dozen cookies.**

LUNCH BOX CARAMEL BARS

- 32 square caramel candies
- 1 (5⅓-ounce) can evaporated milk
- 1 cup flour
- 1 cup quick-cooking oats
- 1 cup chopped pecans
- ½ cup firmly-packed brown sugar
- ½ teaspoon baking soda
- ¼ teaspoon salt
- ½ cup margarine, melted
- 1½ cups plain M & M's Brand candies

Combine caramels and milk in a heavy saucepan. Cook over low heat, stirring occasionally, until caramels are melted and mixture is well blended. Combine flour, oats, nuts, sugar, soda, and salt. Add margarine and mix until mixture resembles coarse crumbs. Reserve 1 cup. Press remaining mixture into a 9 x 13 x 2-inch glass pan. Bake at 375° for 10 minutes. Sprinkle 1 cup M & M's over crust. Drizzle caramel over M & M's. Sprinkle with reserved crumbs and remaining 1/2 cup M & M's. Bake an additional 20 to 25 minutes or until golden brown. Cool slightly. Chill 30 minutes. Cut into bars.

ABOVE: **Lieutenant McGill's tombstone.**

When I was growing up, we all lived on First East; we lived in Anchuca, but at that time it was just 1010 First East. And the Hummels lived on Monroe Street; it wasn't the McNutt Home, just 1706 Monroe. One day my aunt and uncle were taking their three-year-old son to visit the Hummels and they warned him not to ask for anything to eat. "If Mrs. Hummel has anything to serve, she'll serve it; but please don't mention food." He agreed. They went down there and talked and chatted, and she never offered them anything to eat. Finally, the little boy couldn't stand it any longer, he politely asked, "Mrs. Hummel, do you have a kitchen?"

Mary Lou True Halpin

My father, Joseph R. Compton, was born in 1908 and grew up on the corner of Speed and Drummond. He and his friends spent many happy hours planning and designing spectacular candle boxes. They would start with a cardboard box that had a lid and draw designs on the sides and either end. The designs could be anything – dogs, cats, steamboats, cannons, churches, stained glass windows, toys – just whatever struck their fancy. Then they would cut out the designs with their pocket knives. Next, pieces of colored tissue paper were glued inside over the cutouts. A candle stub was anchored in the bottom with hot wax and a hole cut in the lid to let the smoke out. Then a length of string was attached to the front of the box so it could be pulled. When nighttime fell, the children would gather their decorated boxes, light the candles, and pull them up and down Drummond, Chambers, and Cherry Streets.

Dannie Compton Weatherly

When I think of growing up in Vicksburg, I am reminded of the dedication beneath an oil painting of Christ given to the Episcopal Church of the Holy Trinity by Gloria Thames Bottom and her siblings. It says, "To the glory of God and in memory of our happy childhoods."

Clarissa Behr Davis

The Govenor McNutt House

The Episcopal Church of the Holy Trinity

Louis Comfort Tiffany had the recipe for heavenly light.

Six of the stained glass windows in the Episcopal Church of the Holy Trinity were created in his New York studio following that recipe. And along with the other twenty masterful creations in the church's sanctuary, they have bathed generations of christenings, weddings, services of worship, and funerals in tones, shades, and blends which speak to the heart the way "Pie Jesu Domine" speaks to the soul.

It's light so rich you can feel it. It's light so calming that to speak above a whisper is a sacrilege.

Christ Episcopal Church, six blocks north and two blocks east, was the first permanent edifice for Episcopalians in Vicksburg. With the city in the throes of Reconstruction (political) and reconstruction (bricks and mortar), some in the Christ Episcopal Church parish opted to try to create another parish. They moved with amazing speed. In about a week's time in late September 1869 they met, petitioned the bishop, and got his blessing. They wrote the pastor of Christ Episcopal Church, who wished them well. They advertised a meeting and held it. Then, by ballot, the name the Episcopal Church of the Holy Trinity was chosen over St. Stephen's by twenty to fourteen. Before the end of October, the fledgling congregation owned the lot at Monroe and South Streets, where the Romanesque Revival church now stands.

Then, the pace slowed a bit. The first service in the present building was not until Easter Sunday in 1880.

But, by then the hand of fate had intervened.

Although the church was designed from the very start to contain large stained glass windows, who could have known in the planning stages that the array of large windows behind the altar would memorialize founding members? Three of them – Major D. W. Flowerree, William A. Fairchild, and Dr. P. F. Whitehead – all died of yellow fever in September 1878. Two of their widows – Annie Flowerree and Addie Fairchild – died the following year. Only Dr. Whitehead's widow, Irene Cowan Whitehead, lived to see the church completed and consecrated in 1894 with earthly debts fully paid.

All of the windows are amazing; each is worth hours of study, and each one is documented in a work painstakingly researched and written by members Tim Ables and Bobbie Marascalco in 1992.

Tour groups love the church, and opposite the altar end is an array some visitors say they are surprised to find and others say they find reassuring. In a gesture toward healing, funds for the west-end windows were provided for the most part by Union and Confederate veterans who together wanted to honor the memory of their comrades who fell during the Civil War fighting in Vicksburg in 1862 and 1863.

The Episcopal Church of the Holy Trinity is an amazing place. It tells a story of people unified, a people humbled, and a people in awe of the glory of God.

Charlie Mitchell

FALL BAZAAR

Irene Crook died in 1940 but is remembered to this day for organizing the first parish bazaar at the Episcopal Church of the Holy Trinity. She is also still known for her tea cakes and sweet pickles. Today the bazaar doors open to an array of jams and jellies, cakes and pies, and if you get there early, you just might find some tea cakes and sweet pickles.

Quince Jelly
Easy Bread and Butter Pickles
Lemon Poppyseed Loaf Cake
Lemon Pepper Mayonnaise
Raisin Chutney

QUINCE JELLY

5 to 6 pounds quinces
3 cups sugar

Wash and quarter quinces. DO NOT PEEL. Place quinces, including seeds, in a 6-quart kettle. Cover with cold water and simmer gently until soft and tender.

LEFT: **Italian marble baptismal font.**
ABOVE: **Assortment of breads, pickles, and jellies on the reredos in the chancel.**

Drain through jelly bag or strainer to yield 8 to 10 cups of juice. Measure 4 cups of juice into a 6-quart kettle and boil 5 minutes. Add sugar and boil until syrup registers between 216° and 220° on a candy thermometer. Pour into hot, sterilized glass jars and seal immediately with band and lid. Lid will pop when jelly is cooled if it is sealed properly. Four cups of juice yield 2 pints of jelly.

LEFT: Tiffany window given in memory of Mai-De Collier.
BELOW: An assortment of food on the church altar.
RIGHT: The standard Tiffany signature from 1900 until 1915.

EASY BREAD AND BUTTER PICKLES

1   quart kosher whole dill pickles, drained
2   cups sugar
3/4 cup apple cider vinegar
2   whole cloves
1   teaspoon celery seed

Soak pickles in cold water in refrigerator overnight. Wipe dry. Slice pickles and put back in jar. Combine sugar, vinegar, cloves, and celery seed in a heavy saucepan. Bring to a boil and simmer 15 minutes. Pour hot syrup over pickles. Replace top. Turn upside down for 12 hours.

LEMON POPPYSEED LOAF CAKE

1   box lemon cake mix without pudding
1   small box lemon instant pudding
1   cup water
1/2 cup vegetable oil
4   eggs
1   teaspoon almond extract
3   tablespoons poppyseeds
~   Lemon Almond Glaze

Combine cake mix, pudding, water, oil, eggs, and almond extract. Beat with an electric mixer at low speed until combined; then beat at high speed for 2 minutes. Blend in poppyseeds. Divide batter among 3 greased and floured 8 x 3 3/4 x 2 1/2-inch loaf pans. Bake at 325° for 40 minutes or until a wooden pick inserted in the center comes out clean. Shield cakes with aluminum foil after 30 minutes if cakes begin to get too brown. Punch small holes in warm cakes and pour glaze over. Let cakes cool. These freeze beautifully. **Makes 3 loaf cakes.**

LEMON ALMOND GLAZE:

1   cup sugar
1/4 cup water
1   teaspoon lemon extract
1   teaspoon almond extract

Boil sugar and water until syrup forms, approximately 1 minute. Add extracts. Pour glaze over the warm loaf cakes.

LEFT: **Breathtaking wall of windows.**

LEMON PEPPER MAYONNAISE

1½ cups canola oil, divided
1 large egg
1½ tablespoons fresh lemon juice
1 teaspoon salt
1 teaspoon lemon pepper
1 onion slice (optional)
~ Tabasco to taste

In food processor, using the metal blade, put 1 teaspoon of oil and all of the remaining ingredients. Process until well blended, about 30 seconds. Continue processing and add the remainder of the oil very slowly through the feed tube. As the mayonnaise thickens, the sound of the processor deepens (after about 3/4 cup of the oil); then add the rest of the oil in a steady stream.

RAISIN CHUTNEY

4 quarts sour apples, peeled, cored, and chopped
4 sweet green bell peppers, seeded and minced
⅔ cup minced onion
1½ pounds raisins, chopped
1 tablespoon salt
1½ cups brown sugar
~ juice of 4 lemons
3 cups apple cider vinegar
1½ cups apple juice
~ grated rind of 1/2 orange
1½ tablespoons grated fresh ginger
⅓ teaspoon red pepper

Combine all the ingredients in a large sauce pan. Simmer until thick like chili sauce and seal in sterilized jars. **Yield: 5 to 6 quarts.**

ABOVE: **"Sunday Baptizing"** by J. Mack Moore.

Sometimes we get a little carried away with proper etiquette down here. A few years ago I attended the Holy Trinity Turkey Dinner and sat with my grandmother and her friends. One of her friends asked where I worked and I told her I was a realtor. Well, she asked if I would like to sell her house and I said, "Yes, Ma'am." Later that day, I wrote her a letter so she would remember my name and all if she ever decided to sell. A day or two later, I received a lovely letter from her thanking me for my letter. Naturally, wanting her business and wanting to be nice, I wrote her back to thank her for her letter thanking me. Now we just carry on weekly correspondence.

Harley Halpin Caldwell

The first thing we did when we moved to Vicksburg was join the First Baptist Church. A few years ago we planned to attend the annual father-son wild game supper there. We talked it up all week, and finally the big night came. Just as we were headed out of the door, Hardy, our then four-year-old son, looked up at me and asked, "Daddy, what kind of wild games are we going to play tonight?"

Trip Farris

Emma Brown was a very little, very frail, very feisty lady. One Easter Sunday, about 1955, my family and I sat behind her at Holy Trinity. She had on a beautiful yellow silk suit with dyed-to-match pumps and a yellow straw skimmer with a little-bitty brim. Well, Honey, on the hat was a two-foot-tall stick — yellow, of course — with a bird on top. Nobody paid any attention to the service because every time Emma moved the slightest amount, the bird, with its outstretched wings, would sway back and forth. I was fascinated. After church I said, "Emma, you've got to tell me about your hat?" She said, "Well, I went to Kennington's in Jackson to get my Easter outfit. Picked out my suit and shoes and then sat down at the big mirrored dresser to select a hat. When the clerk brought this out, I knew it was perfect. I tried it on, they put it in a box, and I took it home. It wasn't until this morning when I took it out of the box that I knew about that damn bird. It had been way above the dresser mirror in the store!"

Eloise Dabney Lautier

The Episcopal Church of the Holy Trinity

Lakemont

Buying a riverfront building site for a brand new home was close at hand in 1973, when Lakemont, then a ramshackle old house on a lot which was part of the original Vick survey, intervened.

It's too much to say there has been no looking back for the John Wayne Jabour family. But it's not too much to say, as he did twenty-five years after the decision to buy, restore, and then furnish the 1830 home, "Oh, we've looked. Whenever there's been a new home somewhere Becky and I thought we might like, we've looked. It's just that when we got back to Lakemont, there was never enough on the plus side for the other to make us sell and move."

So the Jabours stayed, he a driving force for increasing preservation and tourism in Vicksburg and she a tour guide during spring pilgrimage season and when bus companies call. Together they've shopped for antiques large and small in New York, New Orleans, and, he smiles, Macon, Mississippi. Together, they learned styles and planned decor, arrangements, and colors through research books and by visits to homes in Charleston and Natchez. Together, they've reared a son and a daughter in the home with its museum-quality pieces. Together, as well, they've been host to a ghost.

William A. Lake, an attorney and member of Congress, was the builder of Lakemont. He was successful at many things, but not so great as a duelist.

His widow, perhaps, is the perfumed presence who visits the gallery where she was standing when she got the news. She also gets credit for breaking a mirror in 1975 on the day the home was first opened to the public.

John Wayne remembers the children were small when they first heard their mother tell visitors the story. They wanted to know more. She told them all she knew. "They've lived with it and enjoyed it, knowing there's a presence there, but nothing really to be afraid of," John Wayne said.

Has growing up amid history and exquisite furnishings made Taylor and Lauren different? Their father thinks so, saying there was good and bad – but mostly good. "We made a point of never telling them, 'Don't touch this' or 'Don't go near that,'" John Wayne said. "I think that has helped them recognize fine things and appreciate fine things."

By trade, the Jabour family in Vicksburg have been clothiers, offering top-quality merchandise. And, inside Lakemont, visitors are sometimes struck by how every piece – large and small – seems tailored to fit precisely where it is. Sort of "made for" the spot.

John Wayne said Becky is the arranger. "She has an eye for that." His interest, he said, has been in various styles. But clearly their efforts have complemented each other, preserving the past and forging a family for today.

Charlie Mitchell

A Lebanese Dinner

Vicksburg's large Lebanese community began immigrating up the Mississippi River in the late 1800s. They were astute merchants who earned respect for themselves and their families with hard work and a deep faith. The foods of their past are now an integral part of our present and are served in homes and restaurants throughout the city.

Hummus Tahini
Lebanese Salad
Chicken with Pine Nut Stuffing
Green Beans with Tomatoes
Honey Nut-filled Cookies

CLOCKWISE: **Chicken with Pine Nut Stuffing, Honey Nut-Filled Cookies, and Green Beans with Tomatoes.**

HUMMUS TAHINI

1 can garbanzo beans
   (chickpeas)
3 tablespoons tahini
   (ground sesame seeds
   in oil)
½ cup lemon juice
1 clove garlic, pressed
~ salt to taste

Drain garbanzo beans. Place all
ingredients in bowl of food processor
fitted with the metal blade and process
until smooth. Serve with pita chips and
fresh vegetables.

LEBANESE SALAD

1 head iceberg lettuce
3 green onions
3 tomatoes, quartered
6 sprigs fresh parsley,
   chopped
1 small red onion, sliced
   thinly and separated
1 cucumber, sliced
~ Lebanese Salad Dressing

Tear lettuce into bite-size pieces.
Combine remaining ingredients and toss.
Add Lebanese Salad Dressing to taste.

LEBANESE SALAD DRESSING:

1½ cups olive oil
½   cup lemon juice
1   clove garlic, pressed
3   sprigs fresh mint,
    chopped

Combine all ingredients. Mix well and
pour over salad.

FALL IN THE DEEP SOUTH

TOP LEFT: Bronze, alabaster, and crystal Empire chandelier in the study.
BOTTOM LEFT: 1790s mahogany knifebox with satinwood inlay.
ABOVE: In the dining room, a Regency rosewood china cabinet inlaid with
satinwood.

TOP LEFT: One of a collection of American figural Victorian silver napkin rings beside Chicken with Pine Nut Stuffing.
TOP RIGHT: Federal convex gilt mirror in the parlour.
BOTTOM: 18th-century récamier in the study.

CHICKEN WITH PINE NUT STUFFING

2 cups Pine Nut Stuffing
1 roasting chicken
1/2 cup butter
1 cup water
1/2 teaspoon salt
1 tablespoon cornstarch mixed to a paste with a little water

Prepare stuffing and lightly place in the chicken, including the skin of the neck cavity, allowing for a rice expansion. Sew the opening with coarse thread. Rub the stuffed chicken with butter, wrap in foil, and bake at 375° for 1 hour and 15 minutes. Remove foil and continue to bake until tender and browned. Prepare a gravy by heating the water, salt, and 1/2 cup broth from the cooked chicken in a small saucepan. Stir in the cornstarch paste just before the mixture comes to a boil and continue stirring until mixture thickens. Cut the chicken into pieces and serve on a platter with the stuffing and gravy. **Serves 4 to 6.**

PINE NUT STUFFING:

3 tablespoons butter
3/4 cup pine nuts
1 pound lean lamb or beef, coarsely ground
1 cup rice, washed and drained
2 teaspoons salt
1 teaspoon pepper
1 teaspoon cinnamon
1 1/4 cups chicken broth

Heat the butter in a skillet and brown the pine nuts lightly. Remove and set aside. Add the lamb or beef to the butter and brown. Stir in rice, salt, pepper, and cinnamon. Add broth to meat mixture. Simmer uncovered 5 minutes; then cover tightly and simmer gently for an additional 10 minutes. Mix in the browned pine nuts.

Lakemont

GREEN BEANS WITH TOMATOES

1½ pounds fresh green beans
1½ cups water
¼ cup butter
1 tablespoon sugar
¾ teaspoon garlic salt
⅛ teaspoon salt
¼ teaspoon pepper
1½ teaspoons chopped fresh basil or ½ teaspoon dried
2 cups halved cherry tomatoes

Wash beans, trim ends, and remove strings. Cut into 1-inch pieces. Combine beans and water in a saucepan. Bring to a boil and simmer for 20 minutes. Drain. Melt butter in skillet. Stir in sugar, garlic salt, salt, pepper, and basil. Add tomatoes. Stir gently, cooking just until soft. Toss tomato mixture with green beans. Serves 6.

LEFT: **Magnolia in the fall.**
BELOW: **Dolphin pedestal table and 1820s sofa with Napoleonic Bee fabric in the parlour.**
LEFT BOTTOM: **Liqueur cabinet inlaid with brass, tortoise shell, and mother-of-pearl.**

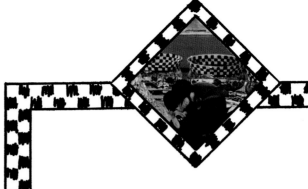

HONEY NUT-FILLED COOKIES

Crust:
- 2 cups flour
- 1 cup butter
- 3 (3-ounce) packages cream cheese
- pinch of salt
- powdered sugar

Mix flour with butter. Add cream cheese and salt. Knead well. Form into balls the size of walnuts. Pat out between 2 layers of waxed paper. Place a teaspoon of filling in center of dough. Bring edges of dough up to center and pinch together to seal. Bake at 350° for 20 minutes or until a light golden color. Cookies will open up a bit during baking to expose filling. Sprinkle tops with powdered sugar. **Yield: approximately 30 cookies.**

Filling:
- ½ pound pecans, ground
- ½ cup honey
- ½ cup sugar
- 1 teaspoon cinnamon
- 1 tablespoon melted butter

Combine all ingredients in a small mixing bowl.

On pretty days I spend a lot of time in my yard, and I see and hear the most amusing things. One particular day, I sort of watched and listened as one of my favorite neighbors, who is of the generation that goes only by Mrs. Frank Everett, got acquainted with a brand new neighbor who was working in her yard. As they exchanged the usual information, Mrs. Everett learned that her new neighbor was a graduate of Randolph Macon College and her husband a graduate of Annapolis. I missed several bits of information, but it was clear that Mrs. Everett was impressed with the lady. Anyway, Mrs. Everett offered her a Coca-Cola. She apparently decided this was her opportunity to show her new neighbor that we weren't a bunch of bumpkins in Mississippi, so she presented the Coke in a sterling silver goblet on a sterling silver tray. I thought to myself, that is Vicksburg and that generation is precious.

Weesie Thames Bexley

This story goes back to the 1920s or 1930s and my grandmother, May Culley, who lived in the 2300 block of Drummond. It seems that a new family moved to town and lived around the corner on Cherry. My grandmother fixed a dish of some sort to welcome her new neighbors and took it down to them and introduced herself. About a year went by and she didn't hear from the nice lady, but she went to a tea one afternoon and the lady was there. She came up to my grandmother and said, "Well, Mrs. Culley, I haven't ever returned the dish that you so kindly brought to me. I apologize, but I frankly forgot about you because I spend most of my time at the Country Club and I have never seen you at the Country Club. Why don't you go to the Country Club?" My grandmother said, "Well, I got out of the Country Club when it stopped being exclusive."

Dick Ferguson

Constitution Firehouse

In Florence, the Ufizi shows off its Michelangelos, its Bottecellis, its da Vincis. In Vicksburg, the Constitution Firehouse shows off its Pajerskis, Comptons, and Whitakers.

Maybe there's a difference, but the principle is the same. Art and the enjoyment of art is the same through the ages and the world over. Art is creative people offering perspectives on a moment, another person, a texture, or a setting or event and communicating those views to others. When it's done well, what occurs is like magic.

Twice a year, the Vicksburg Art Association presents shows of local talent. On opening nights, the house is always packed, the mood is always merry, and the munchies are always, uh, artistically arrayed.

There's something else important to mention about the VAA: It doesn't have any money. For that reason, the Constitution Firehouse, which has been home to this group since 1970, remains pretty much as it was when the last fire apparatus was moved to a more modern facility. It's not that the VAA would have wanted to change anything; it's just that with limited cash, there never has been enough money to think about it.

So today the gallery still has the simple, double-wide wooden doors up front, which could be flung open onto Main Street should the horse-drawn fire

wagon be called into action. The rear features the same arrangement, but that was so the horses could be taken to their stabling area. The unfinished ceiling still shows the ring of framing, now boarded up, through which fire fighters slid down a pole from their upstairs dormitory. The cement floor still bears the etching the powerful steeds needed for traction. As somebody once said, when looking around the spartan accouterments, "If fossil fuels fizzle out and horses are needed in fire stations again, this place is ready."

How old is the Constitution Firehouse? Well, which part? The main building was erected in 1870, but the cupola which makes the building so distinctive – and, presumably, once held a bell with a distinctive peal to summon volunteers – came from an earlier structure one block west. That building went up in 1837, about the time the ink was drying on the 1825 charter which made Vicksburg a municipality.

As will happen, the focal point of city activities has shifted away from Main Street. No longer is it the hub of the community's commerce, residential, and religious life.

But the art is still there. There are student shows, clinics, workshops, and, at least, monthly meetings. Often, there's music. Always, there's laughter. It's an ageless kind of thing.

Charlie Mitchell

VICKSBURG ART ASSOCIATION COCKTAIL PARTY

Mississippi catfish have come a long way, Baby. Used to be it was a lot of trouble to put 'em on the table. You had to have a riverbank, a cane pole, gorgeous skies, bare feet, a leisurely attitude, and your very own time-tested baiting techniques. These days Mississippi farm-raised catfish are as easy to get as walking into the grocery . . . and wondering who's down on the riverbank having such a hard day!

Grilled Catfish Kabobs

Spinach Beggar's Purses

Ham-Stuffed New Potatoes

Sun-Dried Tomato Spread

Fried Grits and Oysters

Cheesy Black-Eyed Pea Dip

Three Chocolate Brownies

Melting Moments

Petites Pralines

FOREGROUND, TOP TO BOTTOM: **Vicksburg houses by Caroline Compton,** watermelon quarters by Jean Blue, and the Old Court House Museum by Elizabeth Pajerski. Pottery by Jeannie Abraham. Spirit sticks by Randy Jolly. MIDDLE: **Buildings by Trudi Green Smith, trees by Hall Whitaker, and still life by Caroline Compton. Firetruck by Earl Simmons.** BACKGROUND: **Red abstract by Randy Jolly, geraniums by Ann Biedenharn Jones, and children in class by Beverly Ferrell.**

GRILLED CATFISH KABOBS

8   catfish fillets
~   Lemon Marinade
~   Soy Marinade
~   lemon wedges for garnish
32 small wooden skewers
~   lemon pepper
~   sesame seeds

Lemon Marinade:
~   juice and zest of 1 lemon
2   tablespoons olive oil
1/2 teaspoon cumin
2   tablespoons white vinegar
1/2 teaspoon red pepper
1   teaspoon lemon pepper

Soy Marinade:
1/2 cup soy sauce
2   tablespoons white vinegar
2   teaspoons brown sugar
1/2 teaspoon ground ginger
2   cloves garlic, minced
1   teaspoon sesame seeds

Wash the catfish fillets and pat dry. Slice each fillet into 4 strips lengthwise. Mix the ingredients for each marinade in bowls large enough to hold half of the fish strips. Add half the fish to each. Cover and refrigerate overnight, stirring occasionally. Before assembling the kabobs, soak the wooden skewers in water and refrigerate for 1 hour to prevent the wood from burning when grilled. Thread a catfish strip on each skewer. Sprinkle lemon kabobs with additional lemon pepper. Sprinkle soy kabobs with additional sesame seeds. Grill over a hot fire for 3 to 4 minutes on each side. Serve warm. Cap each skewer with a small lemon wedge if desired. Serves 16 as an appetizer.

SPINACH BEGGAR'S PURSES

2 tablespoons chopped onion
1/2 cup melted butter, divided
1 (10-ounce) package frozen chopped spinach, thawed
1/4 teaspoon red pepper
~ salt to taste
1 (8-ounce) package cream cheese, softened
2 ounces feta cheese, crumbled
1 package phyllo dough, thawed

Sauté onion in 1 tablespoon of melted butter. Add spinach, red pepper, and salt. Remove from heat. Add cream cheese and feta cheese. Unroll phyllo dough. Stack 3 sheets of dough on work surface. Cover remaining sheets with a damp cloth. Cut dough into 15 squares. Working quickly, place a heaping 1/2 teaspoon of spinach mixture on each square. Fold up edges around spinach mixture and pinch to make a purse. Place on a greased cookie sheet. Continue until all of filling has been used. Purses can be refrigerated overnight or baked immediately. Before baking, drizzle melted butter over purses. Bake at 400° for 10 to 12 minutes until lightly browned. **Yield: approximately 3 dozen appetizers.**

HAM-STUFFED NEW POTATOES

15 small, unpeeled new potatoes
1 cup diced, cooked ham
1/3 cup part-skim ricotta cheese
1/3 cup cream cheese
1 tablespoon minced onion
1 tablespoon Dijon mustard
1/2 teaspoon vinegar
~ paprika
~ fresh parsley sprigs

Place potatoes in a vegetable steamer over boiling water. Cover and steam 15 to 20 minutes or until tender. Remove from steamer and let cool. Cut each potato in half. Combine ham, ricotta, cream cheese, onion, mustard, and vinegar. Spoon ham mixture onto each potato half. Sprinkle each with paprika and garnish with a small sprig of parsley. **Yield: 30 appetizers.**

SUN-DRIED TOMATO SPREAD

2 (8-ounce) packages cream cheese, softened
2 (.5-ounce) packages dried pesto sauce mix
1 tablespoon chopped cilantro
1 clove fresh garlic, minced
1/2 cup sun-dried tomatoes packed in oil, drained well
1/3 cup Parmesan cheese
1 teaspoon dried minced garlic

Mix cream cheese, pesto mix, cilantro, and fresh garlic. Mold into desired shape on serving platter. In bowl of food processor combine sun-dried tomatoes, Parmesan cheese, and dried garlic. Process until combined. Spread over cream cheese. Serve with bagel chips.

FRIED GRITS AND OYSTERS

4 servings of grits
2 dozen oysters
~ juice of 2 lemons, divided
3 teaspoons Tabasco, divided
2 eggs
1 teaspoon Cajun seasoning
~ cornmeal
~ canola oil
~ Salsa

Prepare a 4-serving portion of grits according to the package directions. Spread in a greased 9 x 13 x 2-inch baking dish. Refrigerate at least 3 hours. Drain oysters and add the juice of 1 lemon and 2 teaspoons of Tabasco. Refrigerate. Beat eggs, 1 teaspoon Tabasco, Cajun seasoning, and juice of 1 lemon. Cut the grits into 24 (1 1/2-inch) circles using a cookie cutter. Dip the patties in the egg mixture and dredge with cornmeal. Brown in 1 inch of canola oil. Coat oysters in cornmeal and brown. Place 1 oyster on each patty and top with Salsa. **Yield: 2 dozen appetizers.**

SALSA:

3 tomatoes
1 small yellow onion
1 bunch cilantro
1 teaspoon chili powder
1 teaspoon cumin
~ juice of 1 lemon
~ juice of 1 lime
3 green onions, chopped

Quarter tomatoes and onion and place in bowl of food processor. Add cilantro, chili powder, cumin, and citrus juices. Process until desired consistency. Stir in green onions.

OPPOSITE PAGE: **A Caroline Compton painting of Vicksburg's Main Street with Fried Grits and Oysters appetizers.** LEFT: Paintings, left to right: still life by Jean Blue, street scene by David Baum, child's halloween portrait by Ann Biedenharn Jones, and a Vicksburg corner by Jean Blue. FOOD, CLOCKWISE: **Melting Moments, Spinach Beggar's Purses, Sun-Dried Tomato Spread, Grilled Catfish Kabobs, and Petites Pralines.**

CHEESY BLACK-EYED PEA DIP

1 small onion, finely chopped
2 cloves garlic, minced
1/2 cup margarine
1 (16-ounce) loaf process cheese spread, cubed
2 jalapenos, seeded and chopped
1 (10-ounce) can diced tomatoes with green chilies
2 (15.8-ounce) cans black-eyed peas, drained

Sauté onions and garlic in margarine. Add cheese and stir until melts. Add peppers, tomatoes, and black-eyed peas. Heat thoroughly. Serve with tortilla chips.

MELTING MOMENTS

Cookies:
1 cup butter
1/3 cup powdered sugar
2/3 cup cornstarch
1 cup flour
~ Frosting

Cream butter and sugar. Sift together cornstarch and flour. Add flour and cornstarch to butter and sugar and blend well. Drop dough by teaspoonfuls onto an ungreased cookie sheet about 1 inch apart. Bake at 350° for 10 minutes. Do not brown. Cookies should be white and baked to a melt-in-your-mouth point, not crisp. Carefully remove from cookie sheet and cool. The cookies are VERY FRAGILE! Yield: **5 dozen.**

Frosting:
3 tablespoons lemon juice
3 cups powdered sugar
1/3 cup butter, softened

Combine all ingredients. Beat until creamy. Generously top each cookie.

THREE-CHOCOLATE BROWNIES

1 package brownie mix
1 egg
1/4 cup canola oil
1/3 cup coffee or Kahlúa
1/2 cup white chocolate chips
1/2 cup semisweet chocolate chips
1/3 cup milk
~ powdered sugar

Combine all ingredients except powdered sugar. Spread into a greased 9 x 13 x 2-inch pan. Bake at 350° for 30 minutes. Cool and dust with powdered sugar. Cut into squares.

PETITES PRALINES

2 cups white sugar
2 cups light brown sugar
1 cup evaporated milk
3 tablespoons butter
2 cups perfect pecan halves
1 teaspoon vanilla

Dissolve sugars in milk and bring to a boil over medium heat. Continue cooking, stirring occasionally, until mixture registers 228° on a candy thermometer. Stir in butter, pecans, and vanilla. Continue cooking, stirring constantly, until mixture reaches 236° to 238° on a candy thermometer. Cook without stirring for 5 minutes. Beat with a wooden spoon until slightly thickened and candy coats pecans but does not lose its gloss. Working quickly and using a teaspoon, pick out 1 pecan half at a time and drop onto waxed paper that has been spread over newspapers. When the mixture begins to thicken, it may be gently reheated to thin. Yield: **approximately 8 dozen.**

Constitution Firehouse

McRaven

A ribbon of interstate, an exit onto the main drag of the city, a left turn through three blocks of cottages – some of them looking pretty desolate – and another left just before the railroad tracks. Since McRaven's opening in 1961, countless visitors seeking it probably have gotten precisely this far before declaring themselves hopelessly lost.

The brave among them have believed the signs, forged just 200 yards ahead, and traveled 200 years back in time.

The brave ones have also been the lucky ones. Consistently, no reviewers have said any tour home anywhere affords a visitor better than McRaven a "feel" for the lives of the very real people who settled and built the South.

As a Declaration of Independence was being pondered "up East," stretches along the Mississippi River were being tilled into plantations. Large grants of land had been made by the British in the Colonial era to encourage farming and commerce along the nation's greatest waterway. In 1797, in a settlement which would be called Walnut Hills for another twenty-eight years before being incorporated as Vicksburg, Andrew Glass built the first or frontier portion of McRaven.

After nearly forty years, Sheriff Stephen Howard acquired the property and built the middle, or Empire portion. Thirteen years later, in 1849, what is wispily referred to as the Old South was at its peak. John H. Bobb, later murdered in his own yard, purchased the home and added its Greek Revival portion.

How did McRaven survive the Civil War and the ravages of time? Well, during the actual fighting, McRaven was held sacred as a field hospital, off limits for those targeting cannon fire on the Gibraltar of the Confederacy. The home does bear scars inflicted by random shot and shell, but it wasn't leveled as much of the city was. And after the war, McRaven became home to generations of the William Murray family right up until 1960, when it was purchased, restored, and opened to the public.

It's also true that McRaven's isolated location – away from a through street and nestled behind huge trees and impressive gardens – may have helped save it. Out of sight, out of mind . . .

Oh, those very real people. Leyland French, who purchased the home in 1985 and lives there, knows them like family. Their art, their furnishings, their joys, and their struggles are what he shares with visitors who make it those last 200 yards.   *Charlie Mitchell*

LATE-NIGHT GHOST STORIES AND SUPPER

Vicksburg has famous ghosts and then Vicksburg has local ghosts. The famous ghosts like Mary Elizabeth at McRaven and The Perfume Lady at Lakemont have been on television and the covers of magazines. The local ghosts we're a little less inclined to talk about. But we will talk about the century-old screams we've heard on the battlefields and the plantation bell that rings in the night. Just meet us at McRaven at midnight!

Smoked Chicken and Black Bean Soup

Three-Pepper Quesadillas

Baked Crab Quesadillas

The Very Best Salsa!

Jalapeno Cornbread

Ambrosia Crunch

Oreo Cheesecake

LEFT: **Aspidistra-lined walk.**
TOP: **1856 sheet music, "Belle of Vicksburg."**
BOTTOM: **Sign on the front door.**

SMOKED CHICKEN AND BLACK BEAN SOUP

- ¼ cup unsalted butter
- 1 cup peeled, diced broccoli stems
- ½ cup chopped carrot
- ½ cup chopped onion
- ½ cup chopped celery
- 1 tablespoon thyme, crumbled
- 1½ tablespoons Creole seasoning
- 1½ tablespoons oregano
- 1½ tablespoons basil
- ½ cup dry white wine
- 4 cups chicken broth
- 2 cups broccoli flowerets
- 2 (16-ounce) cans black beans, drained and rinsed
- 1 (12-ounce) can white shoe peg corn, drained
- 8 ounces smoked chicken, chopped
- 1 tablespoon Worcestershire
- 1 tablespoon hot pepper sauce or more to taste
- 2 cups heavy cream
- ~ salt and pepper to taste
- ~ cilantro, broccoli, curled carrots, or croutons for garnish

Melt butter in large pot. Add broccoli stems, carrots, onion, and celery. Sauté for 5 minutes. Add thyme, creole seasoning, oregano, and basil and sauté 5 minutes more. Pour in wine and bring mixture to a boil. Add broth and cook until liquid is reduced by half, stirring occasionally, about 12 minutes. Stir broccoli flowerets, beans, corn, chicken, Worcestershire sauce, and hot pepper sauce into soup and simmer for 10 minutes. Slowly stir in cream and simmer 5 minutes. Season with salt and pepper and serve. Garnish with cilantro, broccoli, curled carrots, or croutons.

THREE-PEPPER QUESADILLAS

- 1 cup thin green bell pepper strips
- 1 cup thin red bell pepper strips
- 1 cup thin yellow bell pepper strips
- 1 cup thin onion slices
- ⅓ cup butter or margarine
- 1 teaspoon ground cumin
- 1 (8-ounce) package cream cheese, softened
- 1 (8-ounce) package shredded jalapeno cheese
- ½ cup grated Parmesan cheese
- 10 flour tortillas
- ~ The Very Best Salsa! (page 103)

Preheat oven to 425°. Sauté peppers and onions in margarine in a large skillet. Stir in cumin. Drain, reserving liquid. Beat cheeses in a small mixing bowl until well blended. Spoon 2 tablespoons of cheese mixture onto each tortilla; top with pepper mixture. Fold tortilla in half and place on a baking sheet. Brush tortillas with reserved liquid. Bake 8 to 10 minutes. Cut each tortilla into 3 or 4 wedges. Serve with The Very Best Salsa!

BAKED CRAB QUESADILLAS

- ⅓ cup butter
- ¼ cup safflower oil
- 1 clove garlic, minced
- ½ cup onion, chopped
- 3 fresh jalapeno peppers, seeded and finely diced
- 1 pound fresh lump crab meat
- ¼ cup mayonnaise
- 1 teaspoon salt
- 1 tablespoon fresh cilantro, chopped
- 16 flour tortillas
- ½ cup Monterey Jack cheese, grated
- ~ The Very Best Salsa! (page 103)

Preheat oven to 475°. In medium saucepan melt butter with oil. Pour all but 2 tablespoons in a small cup; reserve. In remaining butter and oil, sauté garlic and onion over medium heat. Stir in jalapenos, crab, mayonnaise, salt, and cilantro. Mix well. Heat baking sheet in oven. Lay tortillas on baking sheet. Brush liberally with reserved butter and oil mixture. Turn tortillas over. Spread half of each tortilla with crab mixture. Top with a heaping tablespoonful of cheese and fold over. Bake until tops are golden brown and filling is hot, 2 to 4 minutes. Cut into 3 or 4 wedges and serve with The Very Best Salsa!

TOP: **In the kitchen building, an icebox purchased in 1853.** BOTTOM: **Three-Pepper Quesadillas served with The Very Best Salsa!**

THE VERY BEST SALSA!

1 pint cherry tomatoes
2 (10-ounce) cans diced tomatoes with green chilies
1 (6-ounce) can pitted black olives, sliced
2 (7-ounce) cans chopped Mexican green chilies
8 green onions, chopped
3 tablespoons vegetable oil
3 tablespoons vinegar
1 tablespoon garlic salt
1 tablespoon garlic powder
1 cup chopped cilantro (optional)

Combine all ingredients. Refrigerate overnight before serving. **Yeild:** 6 cups.

TOP: **Ambrosia Crunch.**
BOTTOM: **Bedroom in 1797 Spanish Colonial section of the house.**

JALAPENO CORNBREAD

1 cup flour
1 cup white corn meal
1 cup buttermilk
1 (14-ounce) can creamed corn
¼ cup oil
1 large onion, chopped
2 eggs
3 to 4 jalapeno peppers, chopped
2 to 3 tablespoons jalapeno juice from jar of peppers
2 cups sharp cheddar cheese, grated

Preheat oven to 350°. Grease a large cast iron skillet and heat in oven. Combine all ingredients, except cheese. Blend well. Pour half of the batter into hot skillet. Sprinkle 1 cup cheese over batter and top with remaining batter. Top with remaining 1 cup of cheese. Bake for 1 hour. Let stand 15 minutes before cutting. **Serves 8 to 10.**

AMBROSIA CRUNCH

3 cups Rice Chex
3 cups Corn Chex
3 cups Cherrios
2 cups stick pretzels
2 cups peanuts
1 (12-ounce) bag plain M & M's Brand candies
1 (12-ounce) bag peanut M & M's Brand candies
1 (12-ounce) bag white chocolate morsels

Mix all ingredients except white chocolate in a large bowl. Melt white chocolate according to the package directions. Pour white chocolate over the mixture and toss well to coat. Spread on waxed paper and let sit until white chocolate hardens. Store in an airtight container.

Note: Using the Holiday M & M's variety makes this a fun seasonal treat.

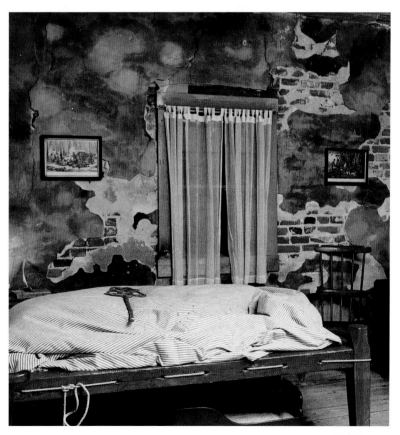

McRaven

OREO CHEESECAKE

1¼ cups Oreo cookie crumbs
⅓ cup butter, melted

Filling:
2 pounds cream cheese
1½ cups sugar, divided
2 tablespoons flower
4 extra large eggs
2 large egg yolks
⅓ cup whipping cream
2 teaspoons vanilla, divided
1½ cups coarsely-chopped
  Oreo cookies
2 cups sour cream

Fudge Glaze:
1 cup whipping cream
8 ounces semisweet
  chocolate chips
5 Oreo cookies, split

Preheat oven to 425°. For crust, blend ingredients in small bowl. Press into bottom of a 9-inch springform pan. Refrigerate crust until firm, about 30 minutes. For filling, beat cream cheese in large bowl with electric mixer until well blended. Beat in eggs and yolks until mixture is smooth. Stir in cream and 1 teaspoon vanilla. Pour half of the batter into prepared springform pan. Sprinkle with chopped cookies. Pour

remaining batter over cookies and smooth with a spatula. Bake 15 minutes at 435°. Reduce oven temperature to 225° and bake 50 minutes. Cover with foil if cake begins to brown too quickly. Blend sour cream, remaining 1/4 cup sugar, and remaining 1 teaspoon vanilla in a small bowl. Spread over cake. Increase oven temperature to 350° and bake 7 minutes. Refrigerate immediately. When pan has cooled, cover with plastic wrap and chill overnight. For glaze, scald cream in heavy, medium-size saucepan over high heat. Add chocolate chips and vanilla and stir 1 minute. Remove from heat and stir until all the chocolate has melted. Refrigerate glaze for 30 minutes. Set cake on platter and remove springform. Pour glaze on cake and spread over top and sides. Arrange Oreo halves around outer edge of cake. Refrigerate until ready to serve.

FAR LEFT: **Oreo Cheesecake.**
ABOVE: **Table set in antique Rose Medallion china on pre-Civil War tablecloth from Boranio, Italy.**
BELOW: **1800s toys.**
OPPOSITE PAGE: **The parlour in the 1849 Greek Revival section of the house.**

FALL IN THE DEEP SOUTH

General U. S. Grant was noted for savoring the spoils of victory, and he was noted as a connoisseur of choice cigars and fine whiskey. His troops often confiscated the best of smoke and drink for him; however, the citizens of Vicksburg were suffering and did not feel obligated to offer gifts. The brave survivors of the siege gathered all of the exceptional whiskey that could be located and poured it into barrels. Instead of hiding it, they buried it. The local undertaker supplied the hearse and the "sad" procession made its way through the ruined streets of Vicksburg to the cemetery. Union soldiers paused as another victim of war passed. With great reverence and veneration, the barrels were interred. This was a perfect plan and it had worked! Years later a group of young soldiers dressed in the familiar grey uniforms were seen by cemetery workmen laughing and yelling as they rode off the hills of the cemetery with the barrels on their horses. The year? 1935, a full 72 years after the siege.

Charles Riles

And then there is the tombstone at Cedar Hills that simply reads, "See, I told you I was sick."

Carole Blackledge Campbell

Vicksburg seems to have more than its fair share of unusual characters – maybe because it's a rivertown – but one such person was the late Corinne Bonelli. To visit her dear, departed husband Albert, she and her poodle Napoleon often walked in Cedar Hills Cemetery. One day the inevitable happened; the dog fell into a freshly-dug grave. Getting him out was a problem for the petite lady, and she did the only thing she could do – climb in! Once in, she lifted the dog and slowly, carefully climbed out. Low and behold, the funeral procession to the freshly-dug grave was arriving just in time to witness Mrs. Bonelli rising from the dead.

Betty Williams Bullard

WINTER IN THE DEEP SOUTH

Winter, to me, has always been a time when faith and hope go hand in hand.

Faith in something that, in the South, is rarely seen. And hope that before winter gently nudges its way into spring, my faith will be rewarded and I'll see it.

Snow. Wonderful, white, fluffy, no-two-alike flakes falling from the heavens.

But, here in Mississippi, winters, like tired Southern gentlemen, tend to tread lightly – frost kissing the ground one day and blowing in 60-degree temperatures the next.

On occasion, winter takes an angry turn, haughtily hoisting heavy layers of ice over the land, leaving limbs to break and cars to slide.

And once in a very blue moon, snow does fall. And it is those delicious, vanilla-frosted days that have given me my fondest winter memories.

Mammaw's snow ice cream – I can close my eyes and still taste the cold sweetness on my tongue. Pounds of sweaters, socks, and scarves. Frostbitten faces, hands, and feet. Snow angels and snowball fights. Hot chocolate and homemade soup. And the crunching sound of snow under your seldom-worn boots.

Surely there are snow memories yet to make in my Mississippi winters to come.

I have hope. And I'm keeping the faith.

Leslie Criss

Leslie Criss is a native of Grenada, Mississippi, who taught high school English before attending graduate school in journalism at Ole Miss. She came to Vicksburg as a features writer for The Vicksburg Post *and was author of a weekly column, "Squaring Off," for almost seven years. She then took off for yet another career – this time the restaurant business. She and her sister own and operate Snickerdoodles in Corinth, Mississippi, and as often as possible she returns to visit her friends in Vicksburg.*

Old Court House Museum

It has been called Vicksburg's wedding cake on the hill. And certainly it's the place to go to enjoy a slice of history.

It has been referred to as Grandma's attic – a place where visitors will surely find some treasure from the past.

The Old Court House Museum.

"It is a place where local folks from down the street or on the corner or out in the country can come to dig for information – and find it," said Gordon Cotton, curator. "Here you'll find some trivial things, some fine things, some not-so-fine things; and all together, they help to tell a story."

The stately building, completed in 1860 by skilled laborers, has its own story to tell.

Housing Union prisoners may have saved the building from destruction during the Civil War.

History has it that orders were given during the siege in 1863 to shell the courthouse. But when the order-giving officer received word of the Union prisoners inside, the building was spared. The clock tower and cupola were the only parts of the building inadvertently damaged during the war.

From the courthouse hill overlooking the city, a young man who dreamed of making a difference made his first bid for public office in 1843. The man's name – Jefferson Davis. County government continued to be conducted from the building on the hill until a new courthouse was constructed in 1939 just across Cherry Street from the Old Court House. For almost a decade the building was left abandoned; upkeep was virtually nonexistent. Until Eva Whitaker Davis took a notion to turn the building into a museum.

With grit and determination, Davis harangued and harassed local officials until in 1947 they finally gave in, holding to the firm belief that Davis would give up her goal in a short time.

They were wrong.

In celebration of Jefferson Davis' birthday – June 3 – the building on the hill was opened on that date in 1948 as a place to house history – the Old Court House Museum. In charge of operating the museum for the Vicksburg/Warren County Historical Society was Eva W. Davis.

Today, visitors and local folks alike still enjoy Davis' unyielding efforts. Outside, visitors are greeted by a breathtaking, bird's-eye view of the Mighty Mississippi. Once inside, a self-guided tour is sure to reveal a clearer picture of the Confederacy. In display rooms throughout the building, a plethora of historic paraphernalia can be found to interest a wide variety of tastes.

Leslie Criss

Book Signing Reception

Name one small, southern town that can be found in any encyclopedia, the dictionary, all United States history textbooks, and virtually every book published about the Civil War. Vicksburg, of course. Vicksburg is a book town – we're in books, we write books, we embrace research for books, and, best of all, we celebrate books.

Vicksburg Brunch Casserole

Squash Robin

Pumpkin Spice Cake with Raisin Frosting

Cheddar Cheese Cookies

Almond Pastry

Festival Fruit Compote

VICKSBURG BRUNCH CASSEROLE

4 cups toasted rice cereal, divided

2 pounds ground sausage, hot or mild

2 tablespoons chopped onion

2 cups cooked rice

2 (10-ounce) packages sharp cheddar cheese, grated

2 (10 3/4-ounce) cans cream of mushroom soup, undiluted

1/2 cup milk

6 eggs, slightly beaten

Grease a 9 x 13 x 2-inch casserole dish. Spread 3 cups cereal in dish. Brown and drain sausage and onion. Layer sausage and onion, cooked rice, and cheese in dish. Combine soup, milk, and eggs. Poke holes all over casserole. Pour soup mixture over top. Sprinkle top with remaining 1 cup cereal. Bake at 350° for 45 minutes.

ABOVE: **Clockwise from left, Vicksburg Brunch Casserole, Squash Robin, Pumpkin Spice Cake, Festival Fruit Compotes, and Almond Pastry.** TOP RIGHT: **Bust of Robert E. Lee with books by Vicksburg's Gordon Cotton and the late Charlie Faulk.**

SQUASH ROBIN

8 to 10 small to medium squash, thinly sliced
~ salt
1 green bell pepper, chopped
1 red bell pepper, chopped
3 large eggs
3/4 cup milk
8 ounces Monterey Jack cheese, grated
8 ounces sharp cheddar cheese, grated
~ pepper to taste

Boil squash and bell peppers together in salted water until soft, approximately 20 minutes. Drain. Beat together eggs, milk, and cheeses. Add squash and pepper. Combine well. Pour into a greased 9 x 13 x 2-inch pan. Bake at 350° for 30 minutes or until set. Serves 12. Freezes well before baking.

TOP: **Where court was held in Warren County from 1859 until 1939.**
BOTTOM, LEFT: **A cotton-bale arch erected for President Theodore Roosevelt's visit.**
BOTTOM, RIGHT: **A quilt collection.**

WINTER IN THE DEEP SOUTH

PUMPKIN SPICE CAKE

1¹/₂   cups butter, melted
2   cups sugar
3¹/₈   cups all-purpose flour, divided
2   teaspoons cinnamon
2   teaspoons allspice
1   teaspoon nutmeg
1   teaspoon ground cloves
2   teaspoons baking powder
1   teaspoons baking soda
1   teaspoon salt
2   cups mashed pumpkin (not pie filling)
4   eggs
2   teaspoons vanilla extract
2   teaspoons rum extract
1   cup chopped pecans
1   cup moisture-added baking raisins
~   Raisin Frosting

Cream butter and sugar. Add 3 cups flour, spices, baking powder, baking soda, salt, and pumpkin. Add the eggs one at a time, beating well after each addition. Add extracts. Mix nuts and raisins with remaining 1/8 cup of flour. Add to batter. Pour batter into a greased and floured bundt or tube pan. Bake at 350° for 1 hour. Spread cake with Raisin Frosting letting excess frosting fill center of cake. **Serves 14 to 16.** Cake can be frozen prior to frosting.

RAISIN FROSTING:

1   cup evaporated milk
1   cup brown sugar, packed
3   egg yolks, slightly beaten
¹/₂   cup butter
1   teaspoon vanilla extract
1   teaspoon rum extract
³/₄   cup shredded coconut
³/₄   cup finely chopped pecans
1   cup moisture-added baking raisins

In a saucepan combine the first six ingredients. Cook the mixture over medium heat for 12 minutes, stirring constantly. Remove from heat and stir in coconut, pecans, and raisins. Let frosting cool.

FAR LEFT: **Pumpkin Spice Cake** on judges' steps in the courtroom.
LEFT: Steiff "Teddy" given by Teddy Roosevelt to a local child in 1907.
TOP: Part of a collection of 334 demitasse cups.

The Old Court House Museum

CHEDDAR CHEESE COOKIES

1   cup butter, softened
8   ounces extra-sharp cheddar
    cheese, grated
2   cups all-purpose flour
½   teaspoon salt
¾   teaspoon red pepper
1   cup chopped pecans

Cream butter and cheese in food processor. Add flour, salt, and red pepper. Add pecans. Roll into balls and flatten with a fork. Bake on an ungreased cookie sheet at 325° for 25 to 30 minutes.

ALMOND PASTRY

1   (17 ¼-ounce) package
    puff pastry
4   ounces almond paste
1¼ cups powdered sugar, sifted
1½ teaspoons lemon juice
~   water
~   toasted almond slices

Remove pastry from package and let stand at room temperature for 20 minutes to thaw. Unfold pastry and cut one 9-inch round from each sheet. Place almond paste between 2 sheets of waxed paper and roll in a 9-inch round. Place one round of pastry on an ungreased baking sheet. Place round of almond paste on the pastry round and top with second round of pastry. Bake at 375° for 20 to 25 minutes. Mix powdered sugar, lemon juice, and enough water to make the glaze thin enough to drizzle, about 1 tablespoon. Drizzle top of pastry with glaze and sprinkle with almond slices. Cut into small wedges. Serve warm or cold. **Yield: 10 to 12 servings.**

LEFT: **View from west balcony, Ionic columns.** BELOW: **Painting from Merci Train.** OPPOSITE PAGE: **Cheddar Cheese Cookies and antique syllabub.**

FESTIVAL FRUIT COMPOTE

12 soft macaroons, coconut if
    available
1   (16 ½-ounce) can pitted
    dark sweet cherries
1   (16-ounce) can pear slices
    or halves
1   (16-ounce) can peach slices
1   (15-ounce) can pineapple
    chunks
1   (16-ounce) can apricot
    halves
1   (21-ounce) can cherry pie
    filling
½   cup peach brandy

Crumble the macaroons and toast lightly at 400° for 3 minutes, stirring twice. Let cool. Drain cherries, pears, peaches, pineapple, and apricots. Sprinkle half of the toasted macaroon crumbs in a 2 1/2-quart casserole dish. Layer the fruits and pie filling over the crumbs. Pour the brandy over all. Sprinkle the remaining crumbs over the top. Cover and refrigerate at least 8 hours. Remove from refrigerator and bring to room temperature. Uncover and bake at 350° until bubbly, about 40 minutes. **Yield: 10 servings.**

Some people will remember that General Dwight D. Eisenhower came to Vicksburg in the mid-1940s. We had a big parade followed by a reception at the old Hotel Vicksburg, and it was there that he announced his candidacy for president. But the part about his visit I will always remember is that he liked the punch we served so much that he asked for the recipe to take home to Mamie. I ran downstairs to the kitchen and told the cooks that I needed it; and they informed me they didn't have a recipe; they just mixed it up. Well, I thought, what are we going to do now? Here's the next president of the United States, and he's asked for this one simple thing and I don't have it. I decided we would just have to figure it out. I told the cooks to get out all the fixings and then sent upstairs for Miss Lola Snyder, the auditor, because she was very precise. Now here we are: Me in my fine dress, Miss Lola with her pencil and pad, all the cooks mixing and stirring, and we came up with a full-fledged recipe. I whipped that little piece of paper up to the General like it had just been downstairs waiting for me all along. He thanked me, and I actually told him it hadn't been any trouble at all! Several years later we printed the recipe for Old Hotel Vicksburg Punch in Vintage Vicksburg. No trouble at all.

Mary Frances Dent Terry

He called it Roses, and when Enroi de Maurice LeBlond sent the painting to America, it was intended as a gift for Margaret Truman, the President's daughter. Instead, it was presented to the Old Court House Museum when the Merci Train paused here briefly in 1949. Laden with presents for America as a "thank you" from the citizens of France for our help in World War II, the train traveled all over the United States distributing the items, usually to museums and college libraries. Miss Truman, informed of the painting by Mrs. Eva W. Davis, museum director, consulted with the artist and then graciously donated it to the Old Court House.

Gordon Cotton

The Old Court House Museum

The Balfour House

To one historian, two things immediately come to mind with the mention of the brick-built, history-filled Balfour House.

The ball. And Emma.

Emma Harrison Balfour, that is.

The noted letter writer and Civil War diarist and her husband, Dr. William Balfour, bought their home at the corner of Cherry and Crawford Streets February 9, 1850.

Though Emma may be mostly known as a woman who documented the human tragedies and triumphs of the fall of Vicksburg during the war, she was truly a multi-faceted woman of her time.

Her talents could easily have made her a sought-after member of any home demonstration clubs that might have existed in her day.

In 1869, Emma took home the blue ribbon at the Warren County Fair for her home-brewed blackberry and native-grape wine. She also won first place for her silk embroidery.

It is through her letters that much of the history of the home, presently owned by Bob and Sharon Humble, is known. In one letter, Emma offered a plan of the home's ground floor and told of the locations of a stable and carriage house, a separate quarters for servants, and a kitchen – all situated in the back yard.

In other letters, she described in detail the circular staircase and later improvements the Balfours made to their home.

During the Christmas season in 1862, the Balfours played hosts to a plethora of Confederate officers and prominent locals who waltzed the night away in dapper uniforms and elegant ball gowns.

As some historical accounts note: "The night was cold, but the house was ablaze with light and the sounds of music and laughter cut through the chill."

It was the first Balfour Ball. And the gaiety of the evening was abruptly interrupted by the announcement that Union gunboats were afloat on the Mississippi River and nearing the City of Vicksburg.

Though that long-ago Balfour Ball was cut short as men left to defend the city, the evening has been re-enacted for a decade now by fun-loving, history-appreciating Vicksburg residents.

As it was often visited by the likes of General Stephen Lee, General John C. Pemberton, and other Confederate greats, Balfour House is also known as the House of the Generals. After the siege, the house was business headquarters for the Union army until the war's end.

An example of the Greek Revival style of architecture, Balfour House is listed on the National Register of Historic Places.

Leslie Criss

1862 CHRISTMAS RE-ENACTMENT

While Emma Balfour gave us a pretty good idea of how we don't want to spend the holidays, her good friend Mahala Roach started a yuletide tradition all of Mississippi still embraces. Putting up Christmas trees! She read of them in stories about Germany and put up her very first tree in 1851 in her home on the corner of Mulberry and Depot Streets.

Cranberry Brie

Turkey and Chutney Rolls

Capered Shrimp, Artichokes, and Mushrooms

Christmas Pinwheels

Ham Balls

Feta Cheese Ball

Delta Point Landing Eggnog

Brandied Chocolate Truffles

Charlotte Russe

CRANBERRY BRIE

1 wheel Brie cheese, 8-inch diameter
1 cup water
½ cup sugar
½ cup brown sugar, packed
1 (12-ounce) bag fresh or frozen cranberries
3 tablespoons prepared horseradish
1 tablespoon Dijon mustard

Preheat oven to 325°. Remove top rind from Brie. Place Brie in shallow baking dish. Bake 15 to 20 minutes or until the Brie is soft and heated through. Combine water, sugar, and brown sugar in a medium saucepan. Bring to a boil over medium heat. Add cranberries and return to a boil. Reduce heat and simmer 10 minutes, stirring occasionally. Add horseradish and Dijon mustard. Spoon over baked Brie. Serve immediately with crackers.

TOP: Clockwise, Christmas Pinwheels, Turkey and Chutney Rolls, Ham Balls, Cranberry Brie, and Feta Cheese Ball.
RIGHT: Front porch with Roman Corinthian columns.

TURKEY AND CHUTNEY ROLLS

4   packages mini-party rolls
    (in aluminum trays)
1   (8-ounce) package cream
    cheese
2   tablespoons mayonnaise
2   tablespoons sour cream
2   heaping tablespoons
    chutney
1   tablespoon champagne
    mustard or Dijon mustard
1/2 to 1 teaspoon curry
    powder
1/2 to 3/4 teaspoon red pepper
2   to 3 tablespoons minced
    onion
1/2 can whole berry cranberry
    sauce
1   pound smoked turkey, very
    thinly sliced

Remove rolls from tray and slice
horizontally. Do not individually separate
rolls. Combine cream cheese,
mayonnaise, sour cream, chutney,
mustard, curry powder, and red pepper.
Combine onion with cranberry sauce.
Divide rolls into two sheets, top and bottom
on work surface. Spread thin layer of
cream cheese mixture on top and bottom.
Layer turkey on bottom half. Spread a
thin layer of cranberry sauce on top of the
turkey. Replace top. With a serrated knife
separate into individual sandwiches and
return to trays. Cover with foil and bake at
350° for 20 to 25 minutes until warm.
Remove foil for last 10 minutes of cooking,
if desired. Serve warm. Can be made
ahead and frozen.

TOP RIGHT: **Delta Point Landing Eggnog
with Confederate saber and officer's
sash.** BOTTOM RIGHT: **Ceiling rosette.**
OPPOSITE, TOP: **Charlotte Russe and
Brandied Chocolate Truffles on the
sideboard.** OPPOSITE, BOTTOM: **Doorway
framed with Ionic pediments.**

CAPERED SHRIMP, ARTICHOKES, AND MUSHROOMS

4   pounds shrimp, cooked,
    peeled, and deveined
2   (14-ounce) cans artichoke
    hearts, drained and
    quartered
2   pounds small, fresh
    mushrooms, cleaned
1   (3.25-ounce) jar capers,
    drained
1   cup tarragon vinegar
1/2 cup vegetable oil
1   teaspoon minced garlic
2   tablespoons Worcestershire
1/2 cup Catalina dressing
1/3 cup Pickappeppa Sauce
1/2 cup sugar, dissolved in 1/2
    cup hot water
1   teaspoon salt
1   tablespoon curry powder
2   tablespoons lemon juice

Combine shrimp, artichoke hearts,
mushrooms, and capers in a large bowl.
Set aside. Combine remaining ingredients
and pour over shrimp mixture. Cover and
refrigerate several hours or overnight.
Drain well before serving.

CHRISTMAS PINWHEELS

1   (8-ounce) package cream
    cheese
2   tablespoons mayonnaise
1/4 teaspoon Worcestershire
3   drops Tabasco
1/4 teaspoon seasoned salt
~   loaf of French bread
~   additional mayonnaise
~   small stuffed green olives

Soften cream cheese. Mix cheese and
mayonnaise. Add Worcestershire, Tabasco,
and seasoned salt. Beat until smooth.
With an electric knife, slice crust off bread;
then slice lengthwise as thinly as possible.
Spread bread slices lightly with
mayonnaise; then spread with a thin layer
of the cream cheese mixture. At the short
end, place a row of four olives, end to end.
Roll up jelly-roll fashion, making sure that
the ends press down to seal in the olives.
Wrap each roll in plastic wrap and then in
foil. Freeze. To serve, cut off ends of each
roll and slice into 1/2-inch rounds. **Yield:
Approximately 30 pinwheels.**

HAM BALLS

1   pound ground, cooked ham
1 1/2 pounds ground sausage
2   cups cracker crumbs
2   well-beaten eggs
1   cup milk
1   cup brown sugar
1   teaspoon dry mustard
1/2 cup white vinegar
1/2 cup hot water
1/4 cup raisins

Grind ham by processing with the metal
blade of a food processor. Mix meats,
cracker crumbs, eggs, and milk. Shape
into walnut-sized balls. Bake in shallow
dish at 350° for 10 minutes. Meanwhile,
combine brown sugar, mustard, vinegar,
water, and raisins. Stir to dissolve sugar.
Pour sauce over ham balls. Bake for 40
minutes, basting often. Freezes well.
Can be prepared ahead and reheated.

FETA CHEESE BALL

1 (8-ounce) package cream cheese, softened
4 to 6 ounces feta cheese
1 tablespoon sour cream
1 teaspoon dried dill weed
1/2 teaspoon oregano
1/4 teaspoon pepper
1 small garlic clove, pressed or finely minced
2 medium green onions, white only, finely minced
~ salt to taste
5 large radishes, shredded
2 tablespoons minced parsley

Line a 1 1/2-cup bowl with plastic wrap. Blend together cream cheese, feta cheese, sour cream, dill, oregano, and pepper. Mix well until smooth and creamy. Add garlic and onion. Add salt to taste. Spoon into bowl. Cover and chill. Just before serving, remove from bowl and, while still wrapped in plastic, shape into a ball. Remove plastic wrap and roll in radishes. Garnish with parsley. Serve with crackers or toasted pita slices.

DELTA POINT LANDING EGGNOG

2 dozen eggs
3 cups sugar
1 1/3 cup Wild Turkey bourbon or to taste
1 pint whipping cream, whipped
~ nutmeg

Separate eggs and divide sugar in half. Beat egg yolks to the consistency of whipped cream. Add 1 1/2 cups sugar slowly, beating continuously. Add bourbon slowly, beating continuously. In a separate bowl beat egg whites until soft peaks form. Slowly add the remaining 1 1/2 cups of sugar, continuing to beat. Fold egg whites into egg yolks. Fill tall glasses, top with whipped cream, and sprinkle with nutmeg. Serve with an iced tea spoon.

BRANDIED CHOCOLATE TRUFFLES

3/4 cup whipping cream
3 tablespoons unsalted butter
1/2 pound semisweet chocolate, chopped
2 tablespoons cognac or other brandy
3/4 pound semisweet chocolate, chopped
~ finely chopped pecans
~ powdered sugar

Bring whipping cream and butter to a simmer in a heavy medium-size saucepan. Reduce heat to low. Add 1/2 pound semisweet chocolate and stir until melted. Mix in cognac. Let stand at room temperature until firm enough to mold, about 3 1/2 hours. Line a cookie sheet with foil. Spoon truffle mixture by rounded tablespoons onto cookie sheet. Chill until firm, about 1 hour. Roll each truffle into a ball. Return each truffle to the cookie sheet and refrigerate. Melt 3/4 pound of semisweet chocolate in double boiler over simmering water, stirring until smooth. Remove from heat. Dip each truffle into melted chocolate. Shake to remove excess. Return to cookie sheet. After chocolate sets, roll 1/3 of the truffles in pecans. Roll 1/3 in powdered sugar. Leave the remaining 1/3 chocolate. Refrigerate until firm. Remove truffles from foil. Store in refrigerator in an airtight container. Can be prepared 1 week ahead. Serve cold.

CHARLOTTE RUSSE

5 egg yolks
1 cup sugar
2 cups milk

2 envelopes unflavored gelatin
1/4 cup bourbon
12 to 18 ladyfingers
~ additional bourbon
5 egg whites
1 pint whipping cream

Beat egg yolks with sugar in medium saucepan with an electric mixer until light and lemon colored. Scald milk in heavy saucepan over medium heat. Add milk to egg mixture, beating constantly. Cook over medium heat, stirring constantly, until mixture coats a wooden spoon, approximately 10 minutes. Remove from heat. Combine gelatin with 1/4 cup bourbon in a small microwave-safe bowl. Microwave until hot and gelatin is dissolved, approximately 1 minute. Add bourbon and gelatin to egg-yolk custard. Stir well. Let custard cool. Brush ladyfingers with additional bourbon mixed with a little water. Line trifle dish with ladyfingers. Beat egg whites until stiff. Fold egg whites into cooled custard. Whip cream. Fold into custard. Pour into trifle dish and chill.

The Balfour House

The Martha Vick House

The owners of the Martha Vick House have searched tirelessly for information on their home's namesake. To their disappointment, they have found little.

"Martha never married. She had no children. She died at fifty," said Bill Longfellow, who, with David Dabney, owns the home built by a daughter of Newit Vick, the founder of Vicksburg. "There simply were no stories about her handed down by family."

Here's what is known about Martha Vick.

North Carolina-born in 1800, Martha and her family moved to Mississippi when she was eleven. When she was nineteen, both of her parents died of yellow fever, leaving behind Martha and twelve siblings.

Martha prized her independence and was a savvy businesswoman, buying and selling land and slaves without the assistance or advice of a father, husband, or brother. The executor of the estate of one of her sisters, Martha was instrumental in the upbringing of two nieces and a nephew.

She also appreciated fine things, a fact attested to by a list of items Martha purchased from a brother. Included in the list are pieces of silver, mahogany furniture, lamps, bookcases, and much more.

In 1830 Martha had the house built on the corner of Farmer and Grove Streets. An example of Greek Revival architecture, the structure has exterior and interior walls of hand-made brick, with plaster covering the interior walls.

Since Martha left her entire estate to her nieces and her beloved sister, Emily, the house was empty of furnishings when it was sold to the Methodist Episcopal Church. It was used as a parsonage from 1858 until 1902.

The doors, windows, mantels, shutters, and the parlor's ceiling medallion, however, are original to the house.

In all, there have been several owners prior to Dabney and Longfellow, who purchased the home in 1983.

For both, owning the Martha Vick House has been a labor of love. In fact, Dabney's fascination with the red-brick house started when he was a first-grader at Grove Street School.

"I walked by the house every day on my way to school – from first grade through the sixth," he said. "The shutters were always closed. It looked like the most deserted place in the world. I was fascinated with the house even then."

It would be years before Dabney thought of the house again. But in 1983, visiting his hometown, he saw a "For Sale by Owner" sign in the yard. Dabney and Longfellow made a phone call, arranged to see the house, and the rest – like Martha Vick's life – is a matter of history.

Leslie Criss

NEW YEAR'S EVE CELEBRATION

Entertaining is business 364 days of the year at the Martha Vick House, but on the very last day of the year entertaining is pure fun. The talented homeowners bring together all the recipes, inspirations, and enthusiasm of an entire year and pack them into one evening designed to close the social season perfectly.

Pickled Black-Eyed Peas

Creole Shrimp

Holiday Ham

Tuzzi Dip

Swiss en Croûte

Eggplant Antipasto

Pistachio Wafers

Best Chocolate Chip Cookies

Black Forest Torte

TOP: **Jester resting on an 1880s English pharmaceutical scale.**
RIGHT: **Clockwise: Holiday Ham, Pickled Black-Eyed Peas, and Asparagus Dijonnaise** *(page 21).*

PICKLED BLACK-EYED PEAS

1/3 cup canola oil

3 tablespoons red wine vinegar

1/4 cup chopped red onion

1/2 cup chopped celery

1/2 cup chopped red pepper

1/4 teaspoon salt

1/4 teaspoon black pepper

2 (15.5-ounce) cans black-eyed peas, drained

~ cocktail rye bread

~ Dijon mustard

Blend oil, vinegar, onion, celery, red pepper, salt, and black pepper. Pour over peas. Toss gently. Refrigerate 24 to 48 hours. Serve with cocktail rye bread and Dijon mustard.

CREOLE SHRIMP

2 cups cider vinegar
2 cups vegetable oil
2 tablespoons Creole mustard
1 cup finely chopped onion
3 cloves garlic, crushed
1 cup chili sauce
¼ teaspoon salt
4 tablespoons paprika
5 pounds shrimp, cooked, peeled, and deveined

1 cup brown sugar
~ pineapple slices
~ maraschino cherries

In large bowl blend vinegar, oil, mustard, onion, garlic, chili sauce, salt, and paprika. Add shrimp. Marinate, covered, in the refrigerator at least 4 hours.

HOLIDAY HAM

1 fully-cooked ham, spiral sliced if desired
1 cup dry red wine
1 cup bourbon

Preheat oven to 325°. Place ham on a wire rack in a roasting pan, uncovered. Heat ham for 18 to 20 minutes per pound. Combine wine, bourbon, and brown sugar. During the last 45 minutes of cooking, pour glaze over ham and baste frequently. For an attractive presentation, cover outside of ham with pineapple slices and cherries. Allow 1/3 pound of ham per serving.

TUZZI DIP

1 pound hot ground sausage
1 (10-ounce) can diced tomatoes with green chilies
2 (8-ounce) packages cream cheese

Brown sausage and drain. Heat tomatoes in saucepan and add cream cheese. Stir until cheese melts. Add sausage. Mix well. Serve in a chafing dish with tortilla chips for dipping.

SWISS EN CROÛTE

1 round of Swiss cheese, 2 inches tall
1 sheet of puff pastry, thawed
pepper jelly
melted butter

Unfold sheet of puff pastry and spread generously with pepper jelly. Place round of cheese in center of dough. Fold puff pastry over cheese pinching dough together and dampening, if necessary, to seal cheese inside the sheet of pastry. Bake at 400° for 20 minutes or until golden brown. Brush top with melted butter, and return to oven for 5 minutes to give a glossy finish.

TOP LEFT: **From back gallery to parlour with portrait of Martha Vick's youngest sister, Emily, in the background.** TOP RIGHT: Creole Marinated Shrimp. ABOVE: Swiss en Croûte on loo table of English burl-walnut with boxwood inlays. Table was originally for playing the game lanterloo. LEFT: Jade glass.

WINTER IN THE DEEP SOUTH

EGGPLANT ANTIPASTO

2 large eggplants, unpeeled and cut into 1-inch cubes
1 tablespoon salt
1/4 cup extra virgin olive oil
2 large onions, chopped
5 ribs celery, chopped into 1-inch pieces
2 green bell peppers, chopped into 1-inch pieces
2 cloves garlic, minced
1 (28-ounce) can Italian plum tomatoes, undrained
1/3 cup red wine vinegar
4 tablespoons tomato paste
2 tablespoons sugar
2 tablespoons capers
1/2 cup stuffed green olives, chopped
1/2 cup black olives, chopped
1/4 cup fresh basil, chopped
1/2 cup fresh parsley, chopped
~ salt and pepper to taste
1/2 cup pine nuts, toasted

Place cubed eggplant in colander and sprinkle with salt. Let drain for 1 hour. Rinse under cold water and drain. Pat dry with paper towels. In large Dutch oven heat olive oil. Add eggplant, onion, celery, bell pepper, and garlic. Sauté until eggplant is lightly brown, but do not brown other vegetables. Add remaining ingredients, except pine nuts, and simmer for 20 minutes. Remove from heat and stir in pine nuts. Serve at room temperature or cold with assorted crackers.

PISTACHIO WAFERS

6 tablespoons unsalted butter
2/3 cup sugar
1 egg yolk
1/2 teaspoon vanilla
1 cup all-purpose flour
1/2 teaspoon baking powder
3/4 cup finely-chopped pistachios, divided
4 ounces semisweet chocolate
2 teaspoons vegetable oil

Cream together butter and sugar. Add egg yolk and vanilla. Add flour and baking powder. Stir in 1/2 cup pistachios. Turn dough out onto 2 sheets of plastic wrap and form into 2 (6-inch) logs. Wrap well and refrigerate for at least 2 hours, up to 3 days. Preheat oven to 350°. Using a sharp knife, cut chilled dough into 1/4-inch-thick rounds. Place 1 inch apart on ungreased cookie sheet. Reshape into rounds if edges become out of shape. Bake for 10 to 12 minutes until edges are lightly brown and cookies are pale golden. Cool on a wire rack. Melt chocolate with oil in microwave until smooth. Dip half of each cookie into chocolate glaze. Roll glazed edge in remaining 1/4 cup chopped pistachios. Return cookies to rack and let stand for 2 hours or until glaze is set. Store in airtight containers. Cookies may be frozen for up to 2 weeks. **Yield: 4 dozen.**

The Martha Vick House

TOP, LEFT: **Tuzzi Dip in the game room.**
LEFT: Scottish mahogany longcase clock made by William McGowan in 1840 and an 1820s side chair from the workshop of Francois Seignoret in New Orleans. ABOVE: French vitrine with collection of crystal cats. TOP, RIGHT: Pistachio Wafers.

BEST CHOCOLATE CHIP COOKIES

1 cup margarine
1 cup butter-flavored shortening
1 (16-ounce) box brown sugar
2 cups sugar
4 cups flour
2 teaspoons baking soda
2 teaspoons baking powder
4 eggs
1 teaspoon vanilla
2 cups toasted rice cereal
1 cup pecans, chopped
1 (12-ounce) package semisweet chocolate chips
2 cups quick-cooking rolled oats

Cream together margarine, shortening, and sugars. In a separate bowl combine flour, baking soda, and baking powder. Alternately mix flour mixture and eggs with butter mixture, adding eggs one at a time. Add vanilla. Mix well. Add rice cereal, pecans, chocolate chips, and oatmeal. Place by teaspoonfuls on an ungreased cookie sheet. Bake at 350° for 8 to 10 minutes. **Yield: about 64 dozen bite-sized cookies.**

BLACK FOREST TORTE

One recipe chocolate cake
1 (15-ounce) can pitted black cherries
1/2 cup, plus 1 1/2 tablespoons, sugar
1 tablespoon water
2 tablespoons cornstarch
6 ounces German sweet chocolate
1 1/2 cups margarine

1/2 cup sliced almonds, toasted
1/2 tablespoon unflavored gelatin
~ cherry brandy, divided
2 cups whipping cream
~ shaved chocolate

Bake cake in four layers. Cool layers. Wrap each layer in plastic wrap and freeze until ready to assemble. Drain cherries, reserving juice. Heat juice with 1/2 cup sugar. When mixture begins to boil, add the cornstarch mixed with water. Cook until mixture thickens and clears. Add cherries. Set aside to cool. Melt chocolate with margarine. Let cool. Stir in almonds and set aside. Dissolve gelatin in 1 1/2 tablespoons cherry brandy in microwave-safe glass measuring cup. Microwave on high until mixture boils and gelatin is dissolved. Cool. Whip cream with 1 1/2 tablespoons sugar until stiff. Fold gelatin mixture into cream.
To assemble cake: Place one frozen cake layer on serving plate. Spread with 1/2 of chocolate filling. Let chocolate harden slightly; then spread with 1/2 of cherry filling. Top with another frozen cake layer. Sprinkle cake with cherry brandy. Spread with 1/2 of whipped

cream. Top with third frozen cake layer. Spread with remaining chocolate filling. Let harden slightly. Top with remaining cherry filling. Place last frozen cake layer on top. Sprinkle with cherry brandy. Top with remaining whipped cream. Garnish top with chocolate shavings.

ABOVE: **Back gallery.**
OPPOSITE, TOP FAR LEFT: **Black Forest Torte on 1670 William and Mary chest.**
OPPOSITE, TOP: **Painting by French artist Frederic Ragot.**
OPPOSITE, BOTTOM: **Antique linen press laden with Dabney family crystal and china.**

Madeleine Dickson, wife of Judge Harris Dickson, had her big dining room table at her Mulvihill home all set with magnificent French china for a special party. Just before dinner the ceiling plaster gave way and the huge chandelier crashed down on the table. Every single piece of china was broken but one. It's hanging in the dining room of the Martha Vick House.

Bill Longfellow

We had parties, charades and weddings. War did not cheat love of its rights. I had a fine party for the soldiers. We made lots of money. I sold coffee at 50 cents a cup with cream in it, and had eggs, bread, breakfast bacon, sassafras tea and watermelons. We had beautiful music. My party was fine. We charged five dollars for a plate of good things. I paid sixty dollars for a pound of good coffee. We had lots of fried sweet potatoes. I gave the money I made to the Confederates.

Interview, WPA source material

Doots Ferguson was the most wonderful cook in the whole world. And I was a young, know-nothing bride. I didn't have very much money, and I was going to cook a turkey for a dinner party. It was a big deal. I had paid a lot of money for the turkey. I read somewhere to put water and the turkey in a Dutch oven and put the top on, shove it in the oven, and not open the oven for five hours. Well, you can imagine. When I took it out of the oven, there was this bird that looked like it had been desecrated. It was awful looking. The legs and the wings were going all kinds of ways. I broke down in tears; I was absolutely devastated. I called Doots and said, "I don't know what to do. I got this bird and I've got this party and I don't know what to do." She said, "Honey, I'll be right over; just have it in a bucket." She came and got that bird; and the next day, just in time for the party, the turkey came back on a silver platter, "garnisheed" – as Darling Doots used to say – and sliced to perfection. I'm not sure when I realized that this kind woman had bought and cooked a new turkey just to save my party and my know-nothing bride pride.

Mary Ruth Smith Jones

The Martha Vick House

Saint Francis Xavier Academy and Convent

On October 25, 1860 – only ten days after six Sisters of Mercy moved into the John D. Cobb House on Crawford Street – an ad appeared in the Saturday morning edition of *The Daily Whig*.

The ad, placed by the Sisters, announced the opening of an academy for young ladies and a school for boys under the age of twelve.

"Both departments will be perfectly separate and distinct, and care will be taken, in each, to ensure to parents and guardians every advantage of a solid and polite education to the children under their charge."

The school opened with seventy girls and boys enrolled for the first semester.

The Cobb House, which served as convent to the sisters and, for a time, as classrooms to their students, was purchased by the parish of St. Paul Catholic Church for $8,000.

The Greek Revival structure was built in 1830.

The building was used at different times by Confederate and Union troops during the Civil War but was restored to the nuns in 1864.

On August 2, 1868, the cornerstone of the new convent was laid. The three-story building was built at a cost of $30,000 and is one of the largest examples of Gothic Revival architecture in the state. Drip stones over the building's windows give the structure a certain flavor of the Elizabethan period.

In 1885, the two-story, red-brick academy building was completed on the corner of Crawford and Cherry Streets. The entire building project, which included an additional floor on the convent for boarding students, totaled $24,000.

The site where O'Beirne gymnasium was completed in 1955 was originally the convent cemetery. The graves were moved to Cedar Hill Cemetery in 1922.

In the span of less than a century, the work begun by the original six Sisters of Mercy expanded from educating a few in extremely close quarters to educating hundreds in buildings that occupied a full city block.

Their work had not been easy. The education of children had been interrupted by war, by two yellow fever epidemics, and an influenza outbreak as well. But with faith – and by grace – they persevered, providing Vicksburg's young people with outstanding liberal arts backgrounds.

In 1986, the Sisters of Mercy sold the academy/convent complex to the City of Vicksburg and relocated to more modern facilities.

Today the complex houses The Southern Cultural Heritage Foundation. Hopes are high that the Foundation will successfully continue the goal of the Sisters of Mercy – to enlighten others through the humanities and the arts.

Leslie Criss

IRISH DINNER

Ever heard of "Punkin' Hill"? Well, it was right here in Vicksburg – east of town. It's where all the bright redheads from Ireland used to live. The potato famine was the cause of Vicksburg's great influx of the Irish. To the city they brought their poverty, but they brought their wealth as well – a strong Catholic faith and an unyielding belief in religious education.

Dilly Salmon Roses

Split Pea Soup

Eye of Round Roast

Red Cabbage Casserole

Mashed Potatoes and Green Onions

Irish Soda Bread

Irish Coffee Meringue Puffs

DILLY SALMON ROSES

1 (8-ounce) package cream cheese
6 tablespoons finely-chopped green onions
4 tablespoons sour cream
2 teaspoons dried dill
2 tablespoons capers, drained
16 slices pumpernickel bread
9 ounces thinly-sliced smoked salmon
~ fresh dill sprigs

Mix cream cheese, green onions, sour cream, dill, and capers in a medium bowl. Cut each slice of bread into three small circles, using a cookie or biscuit cutter. Spread each circle with the cream cheese mixture. Roll one strip of salmon

into a coil and roll a second strip loosely around the first to form a rose. Repeat with remaining salmon. Place a rose on each bread circle. Garnish with dill sprigs. **Yield: 4 dozen appetizers.**

TOP RIGHT: Detail of chandelier in the convent. BOTTOM RIGHT: Dilly Salmon Roses. BELOW: Table set with Split Pea Soup. View of General John C. Pemberton's headquarters.

MASHED POTATOES AND GREEN ONIONS

4 pounds russet potatoes, peeled and cut into 1-inch cubes
2½ cups sliced green onions
1 stick butter
1 cup whipping cream
~ salt and white pepper to taste
~ additional butter

Cook potatoes in boiling, salted water until very tender, about 15 minutes. Drain and mash potatoes. Simmer the green onions in butter and cream. Add green-onion mixture to potatoes and stir until creamy and smooth. Add salt and pepper. When serving, make a well in the center and fill with hot melted butter. The potatoes are eaten from the outside in, dipping each bit in the melted butter. If serving from a master bowl, make a well and fill with butter; dip each serving in the butter as it is spooned. **Serves 8.**

SPLIT PEA SOUP

1 large onion, chopped
1 cup celery, chopped
1 cup peeled carrots, chopped
2 tablespoons butter
1 smoked ham hock
1½ cups dried split peas
8 cups chicken broth
~ salt and pepper to taste
~ three strips bacon, fried and crumbled

Sauté onion, celery, and carrots in butter until tender. Add ham hock, peas, and broth. Bring to a boil. Simmer covered for about 1 hour 25 minutes. Remove ham hock. Purée 5 cups of soup in a blender and return to pot. Add salt and pepper. Serve in bowls and garnish with crumbled bacon. **Yield: 8 servings.**

EYE OF ROUND ROAST

~ eye of round roast
~ seasoned salt
~ black pepper

Bring roast to room temperature. Season to taste with seasoned salt and pepper. Preheat oven to 500°. Cook roast at 500° for 5 minutes per pound plus 10 minutes. Turn the oven off and let the roast sit in a CLOSED oven for 2 hours. Do NOT be tempted to peek as this will completely ruin the roast. The roast will cook well-done at the ends and pink in the middle. **Yield: approximately 2 to 3 servings per pound of roast.**

RED CABBAGE CASSEROLE

1 medium red cabbage, shredded
1 small onion, chopped
3 medium apples, peeled, cored, and chopped
¼ cup red wine vinegar
¼ cup water
2 tablespoons brown sugar
~ fresh ground black pepper
2 tablespoons butter

Grease a large casserole dish. Combine all ingredients except butter. Place in casserole. Dot with butter. Cover and bake at 300° for 2 hours. **Serves 8.**

WINTER IN THE DEEP SOUTH

IRISH SODA BREAD

- 3 cups all-purpose flour
- 1 teaspoon baking powder
- 3/4 teaspoon baking soda
- 1 teaspoon sugar
- 1 teaspoon salt
- 1 cup raisins
- 2 tablespoons shortening
- 1 egg
- 1 cup buttermilk

Preheat oven to 350°. Lightly grease a 1-inch round cake pan and set aside. Mix dry ingredients and raisins in a large mixing bowl. Cut in shortening, using two knives or a pastry blender. Add egg and buttermilk just until all is combined and forms a soft dough. Turn dough out onto a lightly-floured surface. Gather dough into ball and gently knead 6 to 8 turns until dough holds together. Shape in a 7-inch rounded disk and place into greased pan. Cut a 1-inch deep "X" across the top of the bread and bake 45 to 50 minutes or until golden brown. Serve at once. **Yield: 18-inch round loaf.**

IRISH COFFEE MERINGUE PUFFS

MERINGUES:
- 9 tablespoons sugar, divided
- 4 tablespoons dark brown sugar, packed, divided
- 2 teaspoons instant coffee powder
- 3 large egg whites

Preheat oven to 250°. Line 2 baking sheets with parchment paper. Trace 16 3-inch circles on parchment paper to use as a guide for forming meringues. Combine 4 tablespoons sugar, 2 tablespoons brown sugar, and instant coffee. Set aside. Beat egg whites until medium-stiff peaks form. Add remaining sugar and brown sugar to egg whites and beat until stiff peaks form. Fold in sugar and coffee mixture. Drop meringues by rounded tablespoonfuls onto parchment circles. Spread meringues with a knife to fill in traced area. Bake about 40 to 45 minutes or until meringues are dry and lift off the parchment paper easily. **Yield: 16 rounds.**

FILLING:
- 2 cups whipping cream, divided
- 3 tablespoons sugar
- 3 tablespoons Irish whiskey
- 3 teaspoons instant coffee powder
- ~ chocolate curls or chocolate-covered coffee beans for garnish

Beat 1 1/2 cups whipping cream in medium bowl until medium-stiff peaks form. Add sugar, whiskey, and coffee powder. Beat until firm. Place one meringue on plate and spoon a generous tablespoon of filling on top. Top with another meringue flat side down and gently press until filling spreads to edges. Beat remaining 1/2 cup whipping cream and top each meringue with a dollop of whipped cream and chocolate curls or coffee beans. **Yield: 8 servings.**

OPPOSITE, TOP: **Eye of Round Roast, Red Cabbage Casserole, and Mashed Potatoes and Green Onions.** OPPOSITE, BOTTOM: **Table with a view of the convent.** TOP: **Irish Soda Bread.** TOP RIGHT: **Rooftop view from the convent.** BOTTOM RIGHT: **Irish Coffee Meringue Puff and antique silver coffee pot.**

Saint Francis Xavier Academy and Convent

Wahl-Schaffer Cottages

Nestled confidently among three of Vicksburg's larger historical homes - Duff Green Mansion, Lakemont, and Anchuca - the Wahl-Schaffer Cottages serve as a reminder: Good things are found in small packages.

And in the case of the Main Street home, it's a double dose of architectural pleasure.

On the northwest corner of Adams and Main Streets, the Schaffer Cottage, built in the early 1870s, is an example of a Victorian cottage in the style of the Vicksburg shotgun.

The Schaffer Cottage was purchased in 1979 by William Shappley, who renovated the property as a duplex dwelling.

"Of course, later, when I married, I converted the property into a single-family home," said the Vicksburg attorney.

These days, Shappley, his wife, the former Patsy Lefoldt, and their children, Katherine and Will, call the Wahl-Schaffer Cottages home.

Historically speaking, the parcel of land which is 1023 Main Street was conveyed to Louisa Miller Schaffer in 1852. A structure was built on the property sometime between then and 1900. However, much of Main Street was besieged by fire before, during, and after the War Between the States, most likely destroying any structures that may have been built there prior to the present one.

Adjacent to the Schaffer Cottage is the Wahl Cottage.

The property was purchased in 1842 by German immigrants, John and Lena Wahl, who built a home there in 1844. The Wahls operated their family grocery in the front portion of the structure and lived in the rear.

The home proved to be lucky for Lena Wahl, though she credited a thirsty Confederate soldier with her good fortune.

History has it that one long-ago day as Lena baked bread and her young daughter played outside, a soldier sought a drink of water. Leaving her kitchen, Lena joined her daughter outside to draw water for the stranger. A shell shot through her kitchen roof destroying a good portion of the family's residence, but spared the lives of Lena and her daughter.

The Shappley family purchased the Wahl Cottage, a Greek Revival cottage from the Federal period, in 1986.

Today, the two cottages, situated within twenty feet of each other are joined by a glass-roofed solarium with a brick floor. The room was built around a large redbud tree that grew between the two cottages and extended out through an opening in the roof.

The tree, however, did not weather well the temperature changes wrought by an indoor thermostat and, unfortunately, did not survive.

Both cottages are listed independently on the National Register of Historic Places.

Leslie Criss

ALSATIAN DINNER

Many Vicksburgers came from a tiny part of the world that has long been a prize in wars between Germany and France –Alsace-Lorraine. The Lefoldts were just one such family, and their descendants continue to remind us of the very best of both countries.

Blue Cheese Spread
Tomato Basil Soup
Onion and Mushroom Tart
Apple Galette

BLUE CHEESE SPREAD

1 (8-ounce) package cream cheese, softened
3 ounces blue cheese, grated
½ cup pitted dates, chopped
1 cup chopped pecans, reserve ½ for top
¼ to ½ cup dry sherry

Combine all ingredients and shape into a ball. Roll in reserved pecans and chill.

TOP LEFT: Antique whiskey jug from Louis Lefoldt's Levee Street 1800s grocery and saloon.
TOP RIGHT: Assorted cheeses and French watering can.
BOTTOM: Dining room table.

BELOW: Tomato plant in the solarium.
BOTTOM: The courtyard.
RIGHT: From 1019 Main Street to 1023
Main Street across the solarium.
FAR RIGHT: Tomato Basil Soup in Mistral
Blue bowls by Henri of Quimper.
OPPOSITE TOP: Onion and Mushroom
Tart. OPPOSITE BOTTOM: Apple Galette.

TOMATO BASIL SOUP

 8 to 10 tomatoes, peeled,
   cored, and chopped, or 4
   cups canned tomatoes,
   crushed
 2 cups tomato juice
 2 cups chicken broth
12 to 14 fresh basil leaves
 1 cup whipping cream
 1 stick unsalted butter,
   softened
 ~ salt to taste
1/4 teaspoon cracked black
 ~ pepper
 ~ basil for garnish

Combine tomatoes, juice, and broth in
large saucepan over medium heat.
Simmer 30 minutes. In blender or food
processor combine tomato mixture and
basil leaves. This will need to be done in
small batches. Purée and return
mixture to saucepan on low heat. Stir in
cream and butter. Season with salt and
pepper. Continue stirring over low heat
until heated through. Divide soup
among 8 bowls and garnish with basil
leaves. Yield: 8 servings.

WINTER IN THE DEEP SOUTH

ONION AND MUSHROOM TART

PASTRY:

- 4   ounces fat-free cream cheese, softened
- 1   stick butter, softened
- 1¼ cups all-purpose flour
- ⅛   teaspoon salt
- 1   tablespoon fresh chives, minced

Blend cream cheese and butter in food processor using the metal blade. Add flour and salt. Process until the dough begins to form a ball. Sprinkle chives on work surface. Place dough on work surface and roll in chives. Knead dough to incorporate chives. Form dough into an oval about 1/2-inch thick. Wrap in plastic wrap and refrigerate at least 30 minutes. Dough may be made ahead and refrigerated up to 24 hours. Working on a floured surface, roll the dough into a 13- to 14-inch round. Place dough in an 11-inch fluted tart pan, fitting dough into the bottom of the pan and pressing into the fluted sides. Once fitted into the pan, trim the dough 1 inch from the top of the pan. Fold the edge of the dough along the top edge of the pan and crimp. Refrigerate 20 minutes while preheating over to 400°. Prick the bottom of the tart shell with a

fork. Line the shell with foil and fill with ceramic pie weights or dried beans. Bake for 15 minutes. Remove the foil and weights and continue to bake until sides and bottom are barely golden, 5 to 10 more minutes. Cool completely. Remove fluted rim of tart pan and place shell on baking sheet with metal bottom of tart pan remaining in place.

TART FILLING:

- 1   tablespoon olive oil
- 10 to 12 medium-sized white mushrooms, sliced
- 2   large onions, quartered and sliced thinly
- 3   green onions, sliced thinly
- ½   teaspoon cumin
- ~   dash of white pepper
- ~   pinch of salt
- 2   large eggs
- 2   tablespoons all-purpose flour
- 1   cup half & half
- ~   freshly ground black pepper
- ¼   cup shredded Muenster cheese

In heavy saucepan heat oil. Add mushrooms and sauté briefly until softened. Add all onions and continue to sauté. Add cumin, white pepper, and salt. Cover and cook over medium-low heat for 30 minutes, stirring occasionally. Let cool to room temperature. Whisk eggs. Blend in flour and half & half. Pour egg mixture into onion mixture. Season to taste with black pepper. Pour filling into tart shell and top with grated cheese. Bake in 350° oven for 30 minutes or until custard is set and top is golden. Let cool slightly. **Yield: 8 to 10 servings.**

APPLE GALETTE

PASTRY:

- 3   cups all-purpose flour
- 1   cup butter, very cold, thinly sliced
- ½   teaspoon salt
- ¾   cup ice-cold water

Mix the flour, butter, and salt together very lightly so that the pieces of butter remain visible throughout the flour. Add the ice-cold water and mix quickly by hand, just enough that the dough coheres. Cut the dough in half. The pieces of butter should still be visible. This is enough pastry for two galettes. Wrap the dough in plastic and refrigerate for an hour. For one galette, roll half the dough 1/8-inch thick into a shape that fits on a large cookie sheet.

FILLING FOR ONE GALETTE:

- 5   large apples
- ¼   cup sugar
- 3   tablespoons butter, cut into small pieces
- 4   tablespoons apricot preserves
- 1   tablespoon cognac, optional

Peel and cut the apples in half. Core and slice each half into 1/4-inch slices. Chop the slices of one apple and sprinkle over dough. Arrange the remaining slices on the dough, beginning at the outside approximately 1 1/2 inches from the edge. Stagger and overlap the apple slices covering the dough to imitate the petals of a flower. Bring up the border of the dough and fold it over the apples. Sprinkle with sugar and dot with butter. Bake at 400° for 65 to 75 minutes until galette is well browned and crusty. Dilute the preserves with cognac or water. Brush over the apples carefully so not to dislodge the slices. Cut into wedges; serve lukewarm or room temperature. **Serves 10.**

Wahl-Schaffer Cottages

Biedenharn Candy Company

Solidly situated on the downhill end of red-bricked Washington Street is a River City attraction as well known as, well, Coca-Cola.

The Biedenharn Candy Company.

It's the place where, in 1894, the beloved and bubbly soft drink was bottled for the very first time.

The brainchild of Joseph A. Biedenharn, a young candy merchant, the bottling of Coca-Cola would prove to be a windfall for the soft drink industry. It would also be a windfall for the bevy of Biedenharn brothers who acquired franchises to bottle the popular beverage in Vicksburg, Monroe and Shreveport in Louisiana, and in the Texas towns of Texarkana, Wichita Falls, San Antonio, Temple, and Uvalde.

In a letter to the vice-president of The Coca-Cola Company in 1939, Joseph Biedenharn explained the birth of his idea to bottle Coca-Cola.

"...We were operating a wholesale and retail confectionery business and were dispensing Coca-Cola through our soda fountain...consumer demand had increased and was increasing rapidly, as Coca-Cola could only be had in the cities where fountains were dispensing it, the thought struck one day – why not bottle it for our country trade? We were in the soda water bottling game and it was easy to start it going."

Easy Biedenharn, a grandson of one of the seven beverage-bottling brothers, laughs at what he calls the irony of the brothers' success.

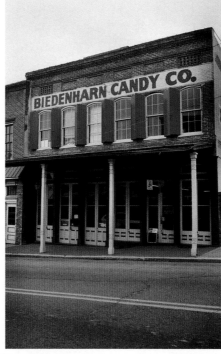

"Of course, the product itself – Coca-Cola – was a success," Biedenharn said. "And the family's affiliation with the product was also a success. You had seven brothers all in the same business. They were all very close, got along well, and could have worked well together in one place. But the reality is that the wives of the seven brothers were not always the best of friends. They just didn't click."

Franchising allowed the young bottlers not only to expand their business possibilities, but to allow for a comfortable distance between families.

"The rest, as they say, is history," said Easy Biedenharn.

In the 1890s, when The Coca-Cola Company began offering distributors an end-of-the-year rebate, the Biedenharn brothers were offered a choice: A $500 cash rebate or stock in the original company.

"Apparently, the family needed the cash – or the story could have been a lot different," Biedenharn said, laughing.

The building where the beverage was first bottled is today owned and operated by the Vicksburg Foundation for Historic Preservation as a museum and is one of Vicksburg's many tourist attractions.

The museum, which opened August 10, 1979, features the historic candy company and Coca-Cola memorabilia, including equipment like which Joseph Biedenharn bottled the first Coca-Cola.

Leslie Criss

BIRTHDAY CELEBRATION

Vicksburgers love to celebrate. A birthday is a grand excuse. Age? Doesn't matter. It's just the living and dining in Vicksburg that counts.

Catfish Canapés
Turnip Green Soup
No-Egg Caesar Salad
Chicken en Croûte
Pecan Rice
Ice Cream Bordeaux

CATFISH CANAPÉS

1   catfish fillet
4   ounces mild goat cheese
2   tablespoons minced sun-dried tomatoes
2   tablespoons minced parsley
1   tablespoon minced green onions
1   dash Tabasco sauce
18 to 20 bread rounds (1½ to 2 inches in diameter)

Poach catfish fillet for about 8 minutes. Drain and cool. Flake catfish. Add cheese, tomatoes, parsley, green onions, and Tabasco. Mix thoroughly. Spread each bread round with the catfish mixture. Place bread rounds on a cookie sheet. Refrigerate until ready to bake, up to 1 hour. Broil for 1 to 2 minutes. Rounds will puff slightly and brown. **Yield: 18 to 20 appetizers.**

TURNIP GREEN SOUP

3   (15.5-ounce) cans white beans
1   (16-ounce) package chopped, frozen turnip greens
2   (14.5-ounce) cans chicken broth
1   pound ham, chopped
2   onions, chopped
3   potatoes, diced
1½ tablespoons sugar
1   clove garlic
~   salt and pepper to taste

Combine all ingredients in a large pot. Add enough water to cover. Bring to a boil. Reduce heat and simmer 2 hours.

NO-EGG CAESAR SALAD

7   cloves garlic, divided
¾   cup mayonnaise
4   anchovy fillets packed with capers, drained
2   tablespoons, plus ⅓ cup fresh Parmesan cheese
1   tablespoon fresh lemon juice
1   teaspoon Worcestershire
1   teaspoon Dijon mustard
~   salt and pepper to taste
¼   cup olive oil
4   cups of ¾-inch bread cubes with crust trimmed
1   large head romaine lettuce, torn into bite-sized pieces

Mince 3 garlic cloves in food processor. Add mayonnaise, anchovies with capers, 2 tablespoons Parmesan cheese, lemon juice, Worcestershire sauce, and Dijon mustard. Process to blend. Transfer to a medium bowl. Add salt and pepper to taste. Heat oil in a heavy large skillet. Cut remaining garlic cloves in half. Add to oil in skillet. Cook until garlic is golden brown, stirring frequently, about 8 minutes. Remove garlic from skillet and discard. Add bread cubes to skillet and cook over low heat until golden brown, stirring frequently, about 15 minutes. Remove cubes from oil and drain on paper towels. Season with salt and pepper to taste. Cool to room temperature. To assemble salad, place lettuce in a large bowl. Toss with enough dressing to coat. Add remaining ⅓ cup Parmesan and croutons. Toss gently and serve. **Yield: 4 servings.**

TOP: **Clockwise, from left: Catfish Canapés, Chicken en Croûte, Pecan Rice, a Catfish Canapé, and Turnip Green Soup. China is Mackenzie-Childs.** BOTTOM: **Catfish Canapé.**

CHICKEN EN CROÛTE

- 8 boneless, skinless chicken breasts
- 2 (17 1/4-ounce) packages frozen puff pastry
- 3/4 pound fresh mushrooms
- 1 onion, chopped
- 2 tablespoons butter
- 1/2 cup fresh bread crumbs
- 1/4 teaspoon thyme
- 1 1/4 teaspoons salt, divided
- ~ pepper to taste
- 1 egg, separated
- 1/4 cup mayonnaise
- 1 tablespoon minced green onions
- 1/2 (10-ounce) package frozen chopped broccoli, thawed and drained well
- 1 egg yolk
- 2 teaspoons water
- 4 tablespoons vegetable oil, divided
- 2 ribs celery, cut into 2-inch pieces
- 2 medium carrots, scraped and cut into 2-inch pieces
- 1 onion, quartered
- 1/4 cup flour
- 1 (10 1/2-ounce) can condensed beef broth
- 1/4 cup Madeira wine
- 3/4 cup water
- 1 bay leaf

Place chicken breasts, one at a time, membrane side up in a resealable plastic bag. Pound very thin, using the flat side of a mallet. Refrigerate until ready to use. Thaw puff pastry according to package directions. Reserve 6 mushrooms. Slice remaining mushrooms. Sauté mushrooms and chopped onion in butter until soft. Add bread crumbs, thyme, 3/4 teaspoon salt, and a dash of pepper. Refrigerate until

ready to use. In small bowl whisk egg white until frothy. Add mayonnaise, green onions, 1/2 teaspoon salt, dash of pepper, and thawed broccoli. Spoon 1 3/4 tablespoons of broccoli filling into the center of each chicken breast. Roll up jelly-roll fashion. Take the first sheet of puff pastry and roll to make somewhat thinner. Cut 8 pieces of pastry large enough to enclose each chicken breast. You will have some pastry left over for decoration. Spread the center of each piece of pastry with mushroom filling. Place rolled chicken breast on mushroom filling; wrap and tuck pastry to enclose. Beat egg yolks with 2 teaspoons water. Use egg yolk to seal pastry "packages." Use extra pastry pieces to decorate — bows, leaves, wreaths, etc. Brush entire pastry with egg yolk. Place in a greased baking

dish. Bake at 375° for 45 minutes. Can be assembled early in the day and refrigerated until time to bake. To prepare sauce, slice the reserved mushrooms and sauté in 2 tablespoons oil. Remove mushrooms. Add remaining oil, celery, carrots, and onion. Sauté 20 minutes on low. Remove vegetables. Add flour to pan and brown. Add additional oil if necessary. Add broth, Madeira, 3/4 cup water, and bay leaf. Add carrots, celery, and onion. Simmer 15 minutes. Remove vegetables and discard. Add mushrooms. Serve sauce over chicken. **Serves 8.**

TOP: **A pretty birthday table setting.**
RIGHT TOP: **No-Egg Caesar Salad.**
RIGHT BOTTOM: **Pecan Rice in cut-glass bowl.**

PECAN RICE

- 1 cup uncooked rice
- 1 stick butter, melted
- 1 medium onion, chopped
- 1 cup pecans, chopped
- 1 (10 1/2-ounce) can cream of mushroom soup
- 1 soup can of water
- 1 (10 1/2-ounce) can beef consommé

Mix all ingredients in a covered casserole. Cover and bake at 350° until rice absorbs all liquid, about 60 minutes. **Yield: 8 servings.**

TOP: **Ice Cream Bordeaux in a gorgeous cut-glass vase.**

ICE CREAM BORDEAUX

½   gallon vanilla ice cream
½   cup crème de noyaux
2   packages Pepperidge Farm Bordeaux cookies, coarsely crumbled
1   cup finely chopped pecans
~   maraschino cherries

Spoon ice cream into a large bowl. Pour crème de noyaux over and fold in. Ice cream will begin to soften. Add cookies and pecans. Mix well. Transfer to a freezer-safe container and freeze 6 to 8 hours before serving. To serve, scoop ice cream into stemmed glasses and garnish with cherries. Kahlúa or kirsch may be substituted for the crème de noyaux.
Serves 8 to 10 generously.

Mother had this wonderful cook named Esterine for about forty years. Those were the days when all the ladies had their bridge clubs at home, about twenty or thirty years ago. Esterine did a beautiful scalloped oyster dish similar to Oysters Johnny Reb in Vintage Vicksburg, *but she had no recipe. Everything was just pinches and dashes of whatever. All the ladies wanted the recipe. So one day, they must have caught her in a good mood, because she gave them the recipe. "You put a little of this and a little of that . . ." The whole smear. They went merrily on their way thinking how much they had accomplished that day. About a week or two later, Esterine was at the Piggly Wiggly doing Mother's marketing, and one of the ladies was in line with her. The lady said, "Esterine, Honey, I did those scalloped oysters just like you told us to, but, you know, they didn't taste like yours." And Esterine drew herself up and said, "I didn't 'tend for 'em to."*

David Hunt Dabney

A lot of people have given memorable parties and a lot of people have attended memorable parties; but you can bet that when one particular party of mine is mentioned, all others seem just a bit trivial. With several other people I was having a 25th anniversary party for German and Judy Jordan. Naturally, I had worked all day long side by side with my longtime housekeeper, Fannie. All the other hosts and hostesses started arriving about thirty minutes before the party hour. As they hustled and bustled on the final touches, I told Fannie to go put her feet up in the den. When the first guests rang the doorbell, I stuck my head around to tell Fannie to come on. There is no way to express the flood of emotion I felt in response to what I saw. Fannie was dead. She had just sat down, propped her feet up, and died. There are a lot of different renditions of what happened next, but I honestly don't remember what took place except mass confusion. Absolutely no one knew what to do. Guests were at the door, Fannie was dead, and, you know, Emily Post just doesn't address these things. Well, we made it through the evening and I will miss Fannie until my dying day; but you can be assured of one thing — no Vicksburgers giving a party with me have ever propped their feet up again!

Marie McGraw May

Biedenharn Candy Company

135

SEASONS IN THE DEEP SOUTH

Blackberry winter is what old timers call the cold snap each year when blackberry briars bloom; it's as certain to happen as cold weather in April if there was thunder and lightning in the daytime in January.

Jonquils are an early sign of spring, their yellow petals on spindly green stems dotting the bleak landscape. They are always prettiest in the pasture, marking an old house site. Soon white iris – flags, our grandmother called them – and then azaleas and daffodils and colorful iris and camellias join them. Redbuds – not red at all, but a smokey lavender – touch the woods like wisps of smoke, along with yellow jasmine and then dogwood, which blooms briefly before its petals fall like snow flurries. There's an urge to till the soil, to plant, but it may be too early. Some trees, like people, cannot resist the hope of an early spring. The Japanese magnolia comes to mind, but never the pecan; it waits until winter's danger is past.

The rainy days of spring give way to the torrid days of summer, when temperature and humidity are both in the upper 90s. Could this be the weather we wished for last winter? The days are counted until homegrown tomatoes are ripe, and gardens yield okra, peas, beans, corn, melons. And squash by the bushel.

Summer's array of flowers begins with day lilies – the old-fashioned "wretched orange" – followed by hybrids in countless colors. And there are hydrangeas – pink or blue or oakleaf white – and roses and calla lilies and dahlias, and hanging baskets filled with ferns. The grass doesn't grow as fast, and we enjoy the afternoons sipping tall glasses of iced tea in front porch swings beneath ceiling fans.

A hint of fall in the air is a welcome respite from the dog days of summer, and soon gum trees turn brown and red and yellow. Some cotton remains in the fields; but there is about as much along the sides of the roadways, and goldenrod decorates the hillsides. Too hot for football, folks will say, but it's sure to be wet and cold at homecoming. It's time for tailgate parties and chrysanthemum corsages. The days are shorter, the mornings a bit airish, and in a few weeks frost will be on the pumpkin.

Winter sometimes arrives early, sometimes not at all. Sometimes it's warm, or maybe miserably cold. Potted plants have already been brought inside, just before the first bitter winds from the north. It's Christmas time, and there's the smell of wood fires, freshly cut cedar, and the beauty of bright red poinsettias. In January, children wish for snow, for school to close, to build snowmen and cardboard sleds; older generations reminisce about making snow ice cream – and long for summer.

Barren trees appear dead, but white narcissus come to life, a reminder that spring is just around the corner. But winter will make one last stand, one last cold blast, when the blackberries bloom.

Gordon Cotton

Gordon Cotton, a native of Yokena, Mississippi, still lives in the same house where he was born. He received his B.A. and M.A. degrees from Mississippi College. He became the director of the Old Court House Museum in 1976. He is the author of several books about Vicksburg and writes a weekly column for The Vicksburg Post, *"Old Court House Comments."*

AMBROSIA STAFF

Editor
Martha Maupin Whitaker

Food Editor
Kimberly Pruette Farris

Design Editor
Suzanne Abraham Hull

Marketing Chairman
Marianne May Jones

Computer Specialist
Cherri Grigsby Campbell

Photography
Bob Pickett
Jeneva Faulk Pickett

Corporate Sponsor Chairmen
Sallie Reid Fordice
Debbie Shows Lewis

Copy Editor
Laurin Fields Stamm

Proof Readers
Patsy Speights Humble
Dani Kay Dottley Thomas

AMBROSIA SEASONAL COMMITTEES

Summer

Virginia Wynne Campbell, CHAIRMAN
Deneen Brown Anderson
Weesie Thames Bexley
Logan Peterson Cauthen
Elizabeth Pugh Halford
Diane Miller Klaus
Debbie Shows Lewis
Camille Barnett Rivenbark
Nancy Cupit

Winter

Mia Smith Cowart, CHAIRMAN
Anne Cashman Cole
Debbie Haworth Collins
Donna Franco Cowart
Lucy Halpin DeRossette
Janet Rogillio Gamble
Teresa Taylor Henry
Lee Evans Tidwell

Fall

Betty Prewitt Penley, CHAIRMAN
Kelly Brown Andrews
Clarissa Behr Davis
Sallie Reid Fordice
Sheila Ward Hudspeth
Gretta Bolden May
Carol Theobald Mims
Mary Lawler Shell

Spring

Nan Williams Green, CHAIRMAN
Harley Halpin Caldwell
Janie Monroe Easterling
Cheryl Windham Nosser
Denise Broussard Sassone
Anita Wootan Webb
Claire Gremillion Weeks
Mille Goodwin Wolfe

CULINARY CONTRIBUTORS
Recipe Contributors

Jeanne Abraham
Linda Cavosie Banchetti
Nan Norwood Barnes
Clara Davenport Behr
Sara Williams Berry
Weesie Thames Bexley
Barbara Walker Biedenharn
Linda Noble Biedenharn
Gloria Thames Bottom
Harley Halpin Caldwell
Cheryl Chapman Cameron
Cherri Grigsby Campbell
Virginia Wynne Campbell
Cissy Wagner Coleman
Debbie Haworth Collins
David Hunt Dabney
Clarissa Behr Davis
Lucy Halpin DeRossette
Janie Monroe Easterling
Story Stamm Ebersole
Kim Pruette Farris
Martha Faye Farris
Janie Selby Fields
Norma Powell Forrest
Heather Burns-Garcia
Nan Williams Green
Christy Boone Guizerix
Elizabeth Pugh Halford

Patsy Hunt Halford
Carolyn Buckner Hall
Susan Maupin Harper
Connie Koury Hosemann
Suzanne Abraham Hull
Elizabeth Parker Jacobs
Hazel Pond Johnston
Marianne May Jones
Mary Ruth Smith Jones
Ellen Evans Kirkpatrick
Diane Miller Klaus
Frances Cox Koury
William A. Longfellow
Sonya Taylor Loper
Janice Cronan Luckett
Corliss Kirby Maupin
Rigby Maupin
Gretta Bolden May
Pam Jabour Mayfield
Beth Ginn Mazzanti
Brownie Burton McGehee
Jan McNeil Milligan
Cheryl Windham Nosser
Mary Oseik
Ann Warren Penley
Betty Prewitt Penley
Josephine Coker Peterson
Jeneva Faulk Pickett

Clara Parks Pinkston
Gail Sweeney Pruette
Carolyn Sasser Ramsey
Camille Barnett Rivenbark
Denise Broussard Sassone
William L. Shappley, Jr.
Mary Lawler Shell
Mary Scott Rosser Shepherd
Nancy Sherard Smith
Laurin Fields Stamm
Kerrie Stephanian
Ruth Porter Stoll
J. Stanford Terry
Jane Andrews Thames
Camille Sanders Thomas
Gayle Ghirardi Tuminello
Peggy Dandridge VanCleve
Penny Sanders Varner
Joyce Harris Walker
Peggy Holder Warner
Wanda Hunt Warren
Anita Wootan Webb
Claire Gremillion Weeks
Martha Maupin Whitaker
Kilby Hickox Whitney
Lois LaBarre Wilson
Patsy Murphy Windham

Professional Chefs

Heather Burns-Garcia
The Duff Green Mansion, Fabergé-Egg Cake

Cissy Wagner Coleman
The Vicksburg National Military Park

Story Stamm Ebersole
Saint Francis Xavier Academy and Convent

DESIGN CONTRIBUTORS

Interiors

Jean Johnson Blue
The Firehouse Gallery

Ann Runyon Carter
The Biedenharn Candy Company

Marianna Robbins Field and Linda Walker Harris
Saint Francis Xavier Academy and Convent

Rick Griffin and Amy Griffin Schrock
The Vicksburg National Military Park

K. K. Hill
*All Saints' Episcopal School and
Wahl-Schaffer Cottages*

Dee Trammell Hyland and Hobbs Freeman
Old Court House Museum

Mary Ruth Smith Jones
Episcopal Church of the Holy Trinity

Ginger Moore Rosser
The Riverfront Park

Peggy Holder Warner
The Corners

Garden

Rick Griffin and Clifton Egger,
Landscape Architects
Ron Carroll

Flowers

Geni Mobley Fulcher and Janet Fairchild
*The Harris Dickson House and
Loosa Yokena Plantation*

Diane Miller Klaus
Grey Oaks Estates

Barbara Walker Biedenharn
*McRaven,
Duff Green Mansion, and
Ambrosia cover*

Nancy Temple Gray
*The Galleries,
The Martha Vick House, and
Cedar Grove*

Mary Ruth Smith Jones and
Claire Gremillion Weeks
Lakemont

Props

Billie Patterson Abraham
Jeanette Thomas Abraham
Kelly Brown Andrews
Carolyn Maly Beard
Shannon Smith Bell
Weesie Thames Bexley
Easy and Barbara Biedenharn
Jane Workman Bodron
Virginia Wynne Campbell
Logan Peterson Cauthen
Donna Franco Cowart
David Hunt Dabney
Clarissa Behr Davis
Joe Gerache
Gold in the Hills
Margaret Bonney Hicks
Lucille Bayon Hume
Jane Posey Giffin

Elizabeth Greer Graham
Nan Williams Green
Syd Johnston
Mary Ruth Smith Jones
Carolyn Walker Lambiotte
Debbie Shows Lewis
Barbara Gilmore Martin
Gretta Bolden May
Carol Theobald Mims
The Miss Mississippi Corporation
Charlie Mitchell
Bonney Bea Neill
Jeneva Faulk Pickett
Carolyn Sasser Ramsey
Regina Rankin
Rachael Elizabeth Sassone
Harry and Alicia Sharp
Mary Lawler Shell
Laurin Fields Stamm
Lee Davis and Jane Thames

Lee Kennedy Waring
Peggy Holder Warner
Dannie Compton Weatherly
Claire Gremillion Weeks
Jo Peterson Wilson
Ellen Maupin Whitaker
Holly Stafford Whitaker
Ann Carter Interiors
Fridge's
Helen's Florist
Latitudes
Olde Tyme Commissary of Jackson
Sassafras
The Collection
The Design Shop
The Ivy Place

Watercolorist

Jean Johnson Blue

BENEFACTORS

We would like to express our gratitude to the following individuals and businesses for their support of this project and the volunteer services of the Junior Auxiliary of Vicksburg.

Underwriters

Anderson-Tully Company
Falco Lime
Fordice Construction Company

Bank of Mississippi
Deposit Guaranty National Bank
Harrah's Casino Hotel
Merchants Bank
Trustmark National Bank

Cappaert Manufactured Housing, Inc.
Entergy
Parkview Regional Medical Center

City of Vicksburg
Columbia Vicksburg Medical Center
Mississippi Hardware Company
Moss Construction Company
Waring Oil Company
West Mississippi Cardiology

Friends

Stuart and Nan Green
Tom and Norma Murphy
Murray and Martha Whitaker

Bobby and Billie Abraham
Gene and Peggy Allen
Dean and Kelly Andrews
Anonymous
Rusty and Nan Barnes
Eddie and Lisa Boleware
Glenn and Virginia Campbell
Frances Cashman
Tom and Anne Cole
Jim and Naomi Cook
Bob and Nell Cunny
Michael and Clarissa Behr Davis
Don and Martha Day
Allen Derivaux, Jr.
Randy and Janie Easterling
Dick and Helen Ferguson
A. J. Buddy Dees, Jr. and Janet S. Fisher
Lee and Norma Forrest
Letty Lassiter Fry
Jim and Margaret Guerriero
Trip and Susan Hadad
John and Joy Ann Hennessey
Lee and Patsy Humble
Guy and Elizabeth Jackson
Ricky and Saralie Johnson
Herb and Mary Ruth Jones
Sonny and Teresa Jones
Howell and Marianne Jones
German and Judy Jordan
Ellis and Frances Koury
Charles and Bobbie Marascalco
Chester and Martha Masterson
Marie McGraw May
Raymond B. May

Robert and Bobbie Jo McConnell
Jed and Joy Mihalyka
Don and Deanna Miller
Robert and Marion Murphy
Mary Dabney Nicholls
Bill and Carolyn Ramsey
Sara Mansell Randall
Robert and Patricia Sadler
Randy and Denise Sassone
Don and Lisa Sessums
Bob and Betty Shell
Stanford and Mary Frances Terry
Ernest and Camille Thomas
Mack and Penny Varner
Ellena Cutrer Ward
Geri Weiland
Edna Earl Whitaker
Robert and Sara Wilkerson
Herb and Faye Wilkinson
Willis and Mille Wolfe
Helen's Florist

May & Campbell Land Company
May & Company
R. R. Morrison & Son, Inc.
The Cinnamon Tree
Varner, Parker & Sessums, P.A.

A special thanks to those people whose ongoing contributions and support could not be easily categorized, but without whom we could not have made Ambrosia.

Barbara Walker Biedenharn
Ed Bohannon
David Hunt Dabney
Shane Fisher
Carolyn Buckner Hall
Jerry Hall
Mary Ruth Smith Jones
Varner, Parker & Sessums, P.A.
Peggy Holder Warner
David Willis

HOMEOWNERS & CURATORS

Our sincere appreciation is extended to the homeowners and proprietors, families, and their staffs who allowed us to photograph their historic homes and sites.

All Saints' Episcopal School
Reverend David and Jan Luckett

Annabelle
George and Carolyn Mayer

Balfour House
Robert and Sharon Humble

Belle of the Bends
Wallace and Jo Pratt

Biedenharn Candy Company
Vicksburg Foundation for Historic Preservation

Cameron Place
David and Cheryl Cameron

Cedar Grove Mansion
Ted Mackey

Constitution Firehouse
Vicksburg Art Association

Duff Green Mansion
Harry and Alicia Sharp

Episcopal Church of the Holy Trinity
Reverend David Elliott

Flowerree
**S. J. (Skip) and Gayle Tuminello
Domonique Tuminello Baker**

Governor McNutt House
Becky Bolm

Grey Oaks
Don and Ann Hall

Harris Dickson House
Robert R. and Natalie Bailess

Loosa Yokena Plantation
John Leigh and Dee Hyland

Lakemont
John Wayne and Becky Jabour

Martha Vick House
**David Dabney
Bill Longfellow**

McRaven
Leyland French

Mississippi Riverfront Park
City of Vicksburg

Old Court House Museum
Gordon Cotton

Saint Francis Xavier Academy and Convent
Dinah Lazor

The Corners
Cliff and Bettye Whitney

The Galleries
Lee Davis and Jane Thames

Vicksburg National Military Park
Bill Nichols

Wahl-Schaffer Cottages
William L. and Patsy Shappley

RECIPES BY CATEGORY

INDEX

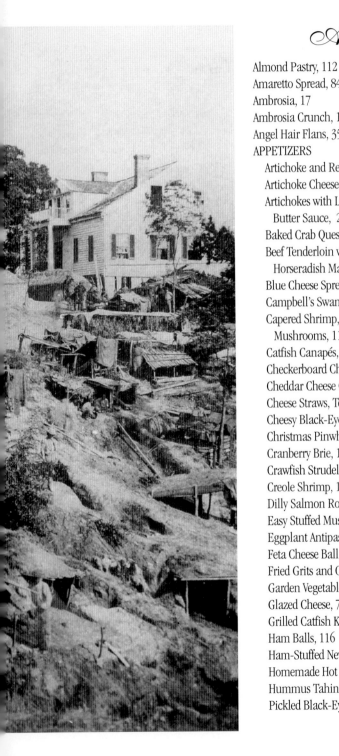

PAGE 8, TOP: **Old Vicksburg family photograph.** BOTTOM, LEFT: **Oil painting at Lakemont.** BOTTOM, RIGHT: **Dressing table at Flowerree.** PAGE 9: **Mississippi Govenor's Mansion place setting with presidential china and state flower.** PAGE 138: **The Valley Dry Goods Company on Washington Street at the turn of the century.** J. Mack Moore. PAGE 139: **Miss Pet Raworth's Day School May Crowning, 1912.** PAGE 140: **The 1927 flood refugee tents at the National Military Park.** J. Mack Moore. PAGE 141, TOP LEFT: **1912 photograph of Levee Street.** J. Mack Moore. BOTTOM: **The old Mississippi bridge under construction, 1930.** J. Mack Moore. PAGE 142, TOP: **Shirley House before restoration, 1900.** J. Mack Moore. BOTTOM, LEFT: **St. Francis Xavier Convent, 1876.** J. Mack Moore. RIGHT: **Grove Street in the early 1900s.** J. Mack Moore. PAGE 143: **Corner of Crawford and Walnut Streets in early 1900s. First Baptist Church on left and City Hall on right.** J. Mack Moore. PAGE 147: **Shirley House during siege of Vicksburg.** PAGE 147: **Turn of the century photograph.** J. Mack Moore. PAGE 148: **1916 Flower Parade.** J. Mack Moore. PAGE 149: **Beginning of the electric railroad, 1890s.** J. Mack Moore. PAGE 150: **Early 1900s parade. Volunteer Southrons marching in front of Yoste Building (present site of Trustmark National Bank).** J. Mack Moore. PAGE 151: **Dining Room, 19th century steamboat.** J. Mack Moore. PAGE 152: **Family photograph taken in the Vicksburg National Cemetery, 1920s.**